# ONE BOTTLE AT A TIME

## A TRUE LOVE STORY

### 50 Tequila Craft Cocktails

DEBBIE MEDINA-GACH

southside *media*

Editing by Cara Highsmith, Highsmith Creative Services, highsmithcreative.com

Cover Design by Maria Godfrey
Photography by Tara Mesler

ISBN-13: 979-8-9916186-0-1
LCCN: 2024920144

Printed in the
United States of America
First Edition
14 13 12 11 10 / 10 9 8 7 6 5 4 3 2 1

# ONE BOTTLE AT A TIME

# PRAISE FOR ONE BOTTLE AT A TIME

"One Bottle at a time is a wonderful and creative collection of craft cocktail recipes for tequila lovers, filled with beautiful photos and easy to follow instructions, making it a must have for any home bar. But this book is far more than an amateur mixologist almanac, it's also a very moving story of love, loss, and perseverance. Each recipe is complemented with a story from Debbie's life. Beginning with meeting her "soulmate" Jonathan, she describes not only the challenges they faced starting a tequila brand from scratch, but their personal journey together as well. Each one of her intimate recollections gives you a true sense of who they were as individuals, a couple, and the bond they shared. Her stories are heartwarming, inspiring, and heartbreaking all at the same time. Cheers to you both."

—Dan Ramm, writer, producer, author

"Debbie Medina Gach has written a wonderful book here. She shares not only 50 cocktail recipes with her (and Joe Mantegna's) top shelf Señor Rio tequila, but a moving tale of heartbreak and loss, recovery and redemption. Pick this up if you like a nice drink recipe and an inspiring story to go with your cocktail. It's the perfect accompaniment. Cheers!"

— Jack Maxwell, actor, TV host, (Booze Traveler)

"Whether you are a tequila lover or just looking for an inspiring story of love and passion, *One Bottle at a Time* will enthrall you from start to finish. This is a personal and deeply moving story of two regular people who met, fell in love, and launched a business based on a shared passion and vision. Life seldom travels in a straight line, and the way Jon and Debbie respond to their challenges will inspire you. If you are a tequila lover, then you are in for a special treat as Debbie has shared a set of unique and delicious cocktails that are reminders of life's lessons."

—Robert Gach, adjunct professor, Fordham University

# DEDICATION

To my late husband, Jonathan, and my father,
Señor Rio, whose vision and passion brought
Señor Rio tequila to life,
this is for you.

# CONTENTS

FOREWORD...                                          ix

COCKTAILS
1. Da Goodfella                                       1
2. Desert Rose                                        5
3. Spicy Lady                                         9
4. Special Friends                                   13
5. Into the Night                                    17
6. A Taste of Mexico                                 21
7. Family Tradition                                  25
8. Big City Paloma                                   29
9. Family Business                                   33
10. Tequila Goddess                                  37
11. Canelo's                                         41
12. Mad Hatter                                       45
13. White Lightening                                 49
14. Labor of Love                                    53
15. What's in your Briefcase                         57
16. Hitting the Streets                              61
17. Charity                                          65
18. Building Blocks                                  69
19. El Señor the Mystic                              73
20. Wild West                                        77
21. La Biblioteca                                    81
22. Scars Earned                                     85
23. Salud, Jimmy                                     89
24. The Pursuit of Happiness                         93
25. Where's the Love                                 97
26. Shanghai Nights                                 101

27. The Situationship 105
28. One for the Road 109
29. Dreams 113
30. Show Ready 117
31. Don't judge 121
32. Above the Stars 125
33. A Dance of Inspiration 129
34. Paper Planes without Peanuts 133
35. Mr. Miami 137
36. Class in a Glass 141
37. Mexican Mai Tai 145
38. Jon's Picasso 149
39. The Frenchman 153
40. No Cigar 157
41. A toast to Jalisco 161
42. Risky Business 165
43. Le Bristol 169
44. Bittersweet 173
45. Lucky 13 177
46. Eternal Spirits 181
47. Tequila Smiles 185
48. Bring Awareness 189
49. The Maxwell 193
50. Da Za Za 197

CLOSING 201
HOW SEÑOR RIO TEQUILA IS MADE 203
INDUSTRY REVIEWS 205
ACKNOWLEDGEMENTS 209
ABOUT THE AUTHOR 210
ABOUT THE COCKTAIL CRAFTSMAN 212
ABOUT THE PHOTOGRAPHER 213

# FOREWORD

As you probably know, there was a famous commercial airing some years ago where the "Most Interesting Man in the World" declared he didn't always drink beer, but when he did, he drank a particular brand. I don't claim to be all that interesting myself, but one thing I do admit to is that I don't always drink spirits, but when I do it's tequila. Therefore, imagine my good fortune when my friend Jack Maxwell who had a wonderful show called "Booze Traveler" dropped my name to the owner of the Señor Rio brand of tequila as a possible partner in her company. Curious as to where this might lead me, I met with Debbie Medina-Gach in Arizona and realized I was now destined to explore yet another new adventure in my life.

You can go on the internet and gather much of the history of Debbie, her father, her husband, and her family, but in reading this book, you'll get all that info in one place; and it's a story that is both tragic, heart-warming, enlightening, and inspiring. Selling tequila is not my day-job; but, after meeting Debbie and having her meet my family, we were all taken by her story and her goal in producing the best possible product in an arena where you can throw a rock in the air and it will land on a celebrity pushing a spirits brand.

I believe in Señor Rio for numerous reasons, but first among them is its three-generations-old commitment to quality and its philosophy of sharing a portion of the success it garners with those who are in need of aid. Having a special needs child myself certainly has made me well aware of the importance of that.

Enjoy reading Debbie's story and give our tequila a chance, I'm assured you'll enjoy both experiences. And you don't have to be the most interesting man or woman in the world to do that, though hopefully it will help you feel that way!

All the best,

Joe Mantegna

# Welcome to One Bottle at a Time.

I am pleased to offer you this collection of fifty tequila craft cocktails, but it is so much more than that. *One Bottle at a Time* goes beyond the bottle and transcends the simple pleasures of a really good cocktail.

I invite you to take a journey with me—one of love, family, fate, entrepreneurship, and loss. I've paired a cocktail alongside each segment of a story that unfolds with every turn of the page. These well-crafted tequila cocktail recipes have their own story and offer a glimpse into my life.

I will share with you how I met my soulmate, Jonathan, who traded New York winters for Arizona sunshine and found so much more. In my own words, you'll learn the why and how we decided to launch an ultra-premium tequila company, Señor Rio Tequila, on a shoestring. You will learn how we grew the company— the sweat equity we invested, the commitment to producing a very special product of the highest quality, and our vision for preserving my father's legacy.

I hope you will enjoy the journey as you mix, sip, and savor each cocktail, and come along on our roller coaster ride into the world of all things tequila.

Guaranteed to put a tequila smile on your face.

A portion of the proceeds from every sale will benefit the compassionate embrace of WeCareCrusade.org. Established in 2021, this foundation stands as a beacon of hope for children with special needs, a testament to the enduring spirit of love and care inspired by my twin granddaughters, Katalina and Klaudia, who bravely navigate the world with Angelman Syndrome.

May the essence of this narrative touch your soul and convey the heartbeat of resilience, compassion, and the transformative power of love. Let the journey begin and let us all contribute to making the world a little brighter—one bottle, one cocktail, one page, and one heart at a time.

To taste tequila is to taste the past.
Reflections of life while mixing it up.

# DA GOODFELLA

## INGREDIENTS

2 oz. Añejo Tequila

1 oz. Antica Vermouth

1/4 oz. Luxardo Cherries syrup

2 good dashes of angostura bitters

Add all ingredients into a mixing glass with ice. Stir 8 times to the left and 8 times to the right. Strain into a rocks glass with a large ice cube. Garnish with citrus peel and a Luxardo cherry.

# I RANG HIS BELL

The year was 2005 and, on that fateful New Year's Day, as most people were recovering from festivities and contemplating their resolutions, I found myself facing an unexpected phone call. The prospect of working on the first day of the year was about as appealing as a root canal; but, little did I know, this call would initiate a chain of events more unpredictable than a game of Twister. The call came from a couple cruising around a neighborhood where I had a home listed for sale. Now, you might be thinking, *Who tours homes on New Year's Day?* Well, most people wouldn't, but these folks were on a mission.

"Hey," the caller said, "We just sold our condo in California, saw your sign, and are interested in the golf course home that you've got listed. Can you show it to us today?" There I was, still in my pajamas, contemplating the age-old question: Do I really want to work? The lure of a potential sale, however, was too enticing to resist. "Sure," I replied, suppressing the urge to yawn dramatically, "I'd be delighted to meet you at the property." As I hastily changed into something more presentable and fueled up on coffee, visions of commission checks danced in my head. I had no idea this seemingly routine showing would lead me down a rabbit hole of unforeseen friendships and adventures.

A time was set to show the golf course property. I arrived early to meet with my potential buyers—a couple in their 30s who seemed friendly and easygoing. They toured the house, nodded apprecia-tively, and dropped the bombshell: "Nice, but not for us." Cue my mental scramble to salvage the appoint-ment. I ran through my listings and selected alternative properties to showcase.

I rang the doorbell of the next home on my list, which was owned by a guy named Jonathan. Picture this: a towering fellow with tat-toos covering both arms, a thick New York accent, and a build reminiscent of Arnold Schwarzeneg-ger. My mind, fueled by an overactive imagi-nation and my over-consumption of mob movies, raced to a lot of assumptions and I started con-cocting wild theories. Witness protection? Ex-con? Goodfella?

We've crafted the "Da Good-fella" cocktail to capture the essence of the vibe I got from Jonathan the first time we met. It's a classic cocktail with a Señor Rio twist, just like Jon-athan.

Desert Rose

# Ingredients

1 oz. Blanco Tequila

1 oz. Lillet Blanc

1 oz. St. Germain elderflower liqueur

1 ½ oz. fresh lemon juice

¾ oz. strawberry puree

---

Add all ingredients into a Boston Shaker tin with ice and shake vigorously. Strain into a martini glass or coupe glass. Garnish with a freeze-dried lemon slice.

# DON'T JUDGE A BOOK BY ITS COVER

Despite my wild speculations, Jonathan turned out to be a stand-up guy who had traded the cold streets of New York for the warm embrace of Arizona. His immaculate home won them over, and they promptly decided to make an offer: full price, with all of the furnishings included. They didn't want to see any more homes on my list.

Back at the office, I sent the offer to Jonathan's realtor and waited with bated breath. The transaction went smoothly, the deal was sealed, and my clients happily settled into their new home, furniture and all. After my clients moved into Jon's home, they contacted him to ask how to use the backyard grill. Jon came over to show them how, bringing steaks to cook for all of them. They became fast friends. At one point, Jon mentioned he had another investment home that he wanted to sell and wasn't happy with his realtor. They insisted he had to go with me. One evening, when I invited my clients to dinner they asked if Jon could join us, thinking it would be a great time to connect us, therefore I could potentially be his realtor too.

Fast forward to a celebratory dinner at Café Roma where I finally got to know Jonathan beyond the tattoos and imposing exterior. Turns out, my Goodfella assumptions were miles off. Jon-

athan was a Fordham University graduate, a former bodybuilder, and an accountant. His move to Arizona was prompted by a breakup, not the relocation of a mob informant.

We learned that we were both foodies. I had gone to culinary school and his dad was a chef in New York, so our love of food was a strong connecting point. As we clinked glasses and devoured Italian delights, I casually mentioned I was changing to a healthier diet, lamenting that this was my last dinner of indulgence—no more wine, cannolis, or pasta dishes for me. Being really into fitness, he asked me about my exercise routine. Since I didn't have one, he suggested that I could train with him at the gym because he worked out daily. Jackpot! How could I refuse an offer like that?

We also connected over being from back East and becoming transplants in the desert. He was kind of a wise guy and I was used to that from Chicago. I embraced and understood his humor, and we came to truly enjoy each other's company.

"The Desert Rose" reflects the lighter side of Jon, who was kind-hearted and playful. He fell in love with Arizona, so we incorporated light, refreshing ingredients to embody an oasis in the desert like Jon was in my life.

# SPICY LADY

## Ingredients

1 oz. Blanco tequila
1 oz. jalapeño infused tequila
1 oz. Lillet Blanc
1 oz. mango puree
1 oz. fresh lemon juice
1 oz. fresh pineapple juice

Add all ingredients into a Boston Shaker tin with ice and shake vigorously. Strain into a martini glass or coupe glass. Garnish with dehydrated mango and a mist of jalapeño tequila from an atomizer.

# THE WORKOUT

My journey to a healthier life-style began with a gentle nudge from my daughter, Crystal. Her concern for my health prompted a profound transformation. I sought guidance from a doctor and embraced strict dietary restrictions, focusing on small portions of meat, vegetables, fish, and eggs.

Teaming up with Jonathan, the former bodybuilder, workouts became a regular part of my routine, and he was a great coach! We walked side-by-side on treadmills for an hour, and that's when we started to really get to know one another just talking about life. Then he taught me how to weight train by doing three sets of twelve reps, working arms one day then back, abs, etc. He enjoyed educating me, explaining how muscles have memory and how cardio is important. He was very encouraging, keeping me motivated, and I was interested in learning. The routine and discipline he cultivated in me fueled my success, culminating in significant weight loss.

Amidst the whirlwind of workouts and shedding pounds, I saw my size-14 frame shrink to a size 4, feeling fantastic, grateful, and full of an abundance of energy. That random New Year's Day showing not only led to a sale but opened the door to a new friendship and a healthier, happier me.

Proud of my achievement, I celebrated with a trip to Disney World in Orlando, Florida, where I crossed off an item from my bucket list by skydiving. Landing safely, I felt an indescribable rush, a feeling of conquering the world.

"Spicy Lady" has a kick to it like our budding relationship at this time. The fruit and spice blend together mirroring the essence of the vibrance and spice Jon brought to everything in life, and especially our time together, celebrating my transformation

# *Ingredients*

1 ½ oz. Reposado tequila

1 oz. Lillet Blanc

1 oz. Ancho Reyes liqueur

2 oz. fresh lemon juice

1 oz. prickly pear syrup

Add all ingredients into a Boston Shaker tin with ice and shake vigorously. Strain into a rocks glass with brown sugar on the side of the glass. Garnish with dehydrated lime.

# The Hot Tub

My blossoming friendship with Jonathan unfolded in many facets. He stepped into multiple roles in my life—accountant, friend, client, and trainer. Our connection deepened as we spent more time together, blurring the lines between friendship and something more.

One evening, I took a leap, both figuratively and literally, when I invited Jonathan into my hot tub and into a new realm. "Do you invite all your friends here?" he teased. "Only special ones," I replied, signaling a shift in our relationship. We continued training, then officially began dating, and soon I was meeting his family in New York.

Jon and his mother, who lived in Arizona in a retirement community, were planning a trip back home to New York to spend time with the family. His brother and his family, and his sister and her husband lived there. I had never been to New York City, so he asked me one day if I'd like to go to New York with them. Of course, I said yes and I met all of them on that trip. It was an exciting time and a significant step in our relationship.

The family reunion in Manhattan, exploring Central Park, and dancing in a techno club created cherished memories. We embraced the youthful joy that being together evoked for us, and exploring his roots in Mount Kisco added a personal touch to our adventures in the city.

Our journey, initially about physical transformation, morphed into a love story.

Our relationship was leveling up and so is this "Special Friends" cocktail. The aged tequila paired with the other ingredients we use evokes a romantic feeling by bringing a little heat to the lips.

# Into The Night

## Ingredients

2 oz. Añejo tequila

1 oz. amaretto

1 oz. fresh lemon juice

1 tsp. Luxardo cherry syrup

2 dashes of Angostura bitters

Add all ingredients into a mixing glass with ice. Stir 8 times to the left and 8 times to the right. Strain into a rocks glass with a large ice cube. Garnish with smoked salt and smoke with a Flavor Blaster.

# IT'S A MAYBACH KINDA DAY

Jonathan was a natural conversationalist and could charm anyone, even the doorman at the Mandarin Oriental where we stayed during our visit to New York, leading to unexpected indulgences and glimpses of Manhattan's glamour.

As we headed out for an evening in the city that never sleeps, we received a surprising offer from the doorman: a luxurious car service for the night. Jon, always up for an adventure, accepted with gratitude, and we were whisked away in a sleek Maybach.

We marveled at the extravagance of the car, complete with built-in curtains, and my curiosity led me to inquire about the purpose for this feature. The driver, with a New York coolness, revealed that they often provide privacy for celebrities and even mobsters. Amused, I closed the curtains, joking about avoiding an onslaught of adoring fans.

My curiosity was piqued further, and I asked about the famous people the driver had chauffeured. He shared a treasure trove of photos, mostly of athletes, sparking a fun conversation during our ride. We had a reservation with his family at Le Bernardin, a French restaurant in New York owned by Eric Ripert, so it was a special night out, and the chauffeured car was a great addition.

Exiting the Maybach into the glittering Manhattan night, an idea struck me. I wanted a picture to capture the moment. We posed in front of the car, dreaming big amidst the city's grandeur. Whether fame awaited us or not, that night felt like a chapter from our own New York tale, filled with unexpected luxuries and the thrill of limitless possibilities.

The "Into the Night" cocktail is everything you want for a laid-back evening in or a vibrant night out on the town. It's smoky and rich with a stronger flavor for the gentleman in your life.

# A Taste of Mexico

## Ingredients

2 oz. Reposado tequila

1 oz. Mezcal Del Maguey

1 oz. fresh lemon juice

2 dashes Angostura bitters

2 dashes orange bitters

Add all ingredients into a mixing glass with ice. Stir 8 times to the left and 8 times to the right. Strain into a rocks glass with a large ice cube. Garnish with a dehydrated lime.

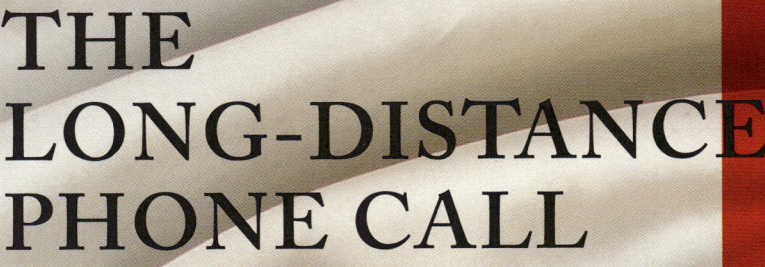

# THE LONG-DISTANCE PHONE CALL

One ordinary day, the unexpected ring of the phone shattered the quiet routine of my life. My father, a distant figure from my past, reached out from Mexico after more than thirty years of silence. Shock and surprise paralyzed me. I was unsure of how to respond to the reemergence of a long-lost piece of my story. His voice, filled with a mixture of nostalgia and longing, carried a simple yet profound request: he wanted to see me. The gravity of the moment weighed heavily on me, and I hesitated, telling him I needed time to think about it.

That evening, I shared the news with Jonathan, who was now my partner in life's adventures. His response was a mix of curiosity and concern, "Your dad? You never talk about him. Are you going to see him?"

Swept up in a flood of emotions, I entertained the possibility. I contemplated a journey to Mexico to reunite with a part of my history.

Jonathan, having lost his father at a young age, empathetically encouraged me to make the trip, suggesting that perhaps my father was reaching out because of something urgent, like illness.

With a newfound determination, I decided to embark on this emotional journey and Jonathan, ever supportive, agreed to accompany me. So, we boarded a flight to Mexico, ready to face the uncertainties that awaited me.

"A Taste of Mexico" blends old traditions with new, bringing in both mezcal and tequila with orange bitters. Jon was a classic good guy, bringing a love for life and discovery that kept things fresh and new.

# Family Tradition

2 oz. Blanco tequila

1 oz. Pierre Ferrand Orange Dry Curacao liqueur

1 oz. fresh lemon juice

1 oz. agave syrup

2 dashes of Fee Brothers orange bitters

1 tsp. of activated charcoal

Dress a margarita glass with lemon juice in a straight horizontal line and dust with Classic Tajin seasoning. Add all ingredients into a Boston Shaker tin with ice and shake vigorously. Strain into prepared margarita glass with ice.

# A Family Reunion

When we finally met my father at his home, emotions ran high.

The reunion was both beautiful and awkward as we embraced. We were more than strangers, but less than acquaintances. Trying to reconnect after decades apart and looking for common ground, my father nervously offered us tequila—a gesture of hospitality that transcended words. He set a simple bottle, devoid of labels, on the table. He poured, we sipped, and the ice broke with the aid of this potent elixir.

In the warm glow of his kitchen, stories began to flow. Confessions and revelations punctuated the air, the tequila acting as a lubricant for opening up and sharing our lives. We talked, laughed, and, admittedly, drank more than intended. No judgments, just the three of us navigating the tangled threads of our shared history.

He unveiled the secrets behind his homemade and natural tequila—a family tradition passed down through three generations, akin to a moonshine legacy. The next morning, as the dawn painted the sky, Jonathan and I were met with a surprising revelation. In spite of how much we consumed, we had no headache, no hangover. The tequila, a testament to his craftsmanship, was not just alcohol; it was a bridge that spanned the gap of lost years.

Our trip to Mexico became a pivotal first page of many chapters to come. The idea of reconnecting with my roots and embracing the unexpected twists of life took hold, setting the stage for a journey filled with tequila-fueled conversations, family stories, and the promise of shared adventures. Little did we know, this trip would plant the seed for a venture that would redefine our paths entirely, preparing the ground for the birth of Señor Rio.

The "Family Tradition" cocktail brings in the elements of celebration with a margarita that has a modern twist with new elements to indicate the ever-growing and ever-changing nature of families bound by generational connections and history.

# Big City Paloma

## Ingredients

2 oz. Blanco tequila
1 oz. fresh lemon juice
1 oz. peach puree
4 oz. Squirt soda or Jarritos grapefruit soda

---

Add the first three ingredients into a Boston Shaker tin with ice and shake vigorously. Garnish the side of the glass with kosher salt. Strain into a Collins glass with ice. Pour grapefruit soda to fill glass. Garnish with a dehydrated lime slice

# LEAP OF FAITH

Back in Arizona, Jonathan and I were inspired by the idea of sharing my father's artisanal tequila with the world.

The real estate industry was facing challenges with a declining market, foreclosures, and short sales, and I felt myself being pushed toward new opportunities. Knowing my real estate background of over two decades—starting in Chicago and later moving to Arizona—provided me with valuable experience, I felt this tequila company might be exactly what I was supposed to do next.

Seeing a gap in the market for fine sipping options, we felt compelled to bring this hidden gem to others. My father lacked the means for large-scale production and many questions lingered: Where do we start? How do we pull this off? Should we take this leap of faith? But we were driven by the belief in limitless possibilities and set out on this tequila-filled journey together.

After twenty-five years in New York as an accountant, Jonathan had moved to Arizona for a semi-retired lifestyle. As we spent more and more time together, I discovered his caring nature and realized that our partnership could be the foundation for something extraordinary.

Our backgrounds and shared vision converged, leading us to explore the intricacies of the tequila industry. With determination and a sense of purpose, we were ready to embark on this new chapter in our lives, blending entrepreneurship with a passion for quality and craftsmanship.

The "Big City Paloma" cocktail is a little "extra" with the addition of peach puree, reflective of how our lives were on the verge of becoming a bit extra as well.

# The Family Business

## Ingredients

2 oz. Reposado tequila

1 oz. Pomegranate juice

½ oz. fresh pineapple juice

1 oz. prickly pear syrup

Add all ingredients into a Boston Shaker tin with ice and shake vigorously. Strain into a rocks glass with a large ice cube. Garnish with a lemon peel.

# *Legacy*

As Jon and I immersed ourselves in the world of tequila, our days were filled with research and communication with distilleries in Mexico. Jon discovered he was skilled in distillery relations and contacted tequila makers in Mexico. I scoured the internet to gain more knowledge about tequila. Together, we navigated the complexities of this new business venture, determined to craft a tequila that mirrored the smoothness and flavor of my father's family recipe in a way that was scalable.

Our journey led us to Jalisco, the heart of tequila country, in search of a distillery aligned with our vision. Many offered generic stock tequila, but we sought something unique—a sippable masterpiece like my father's. The tequila-making process unfolded like a captivating adventure, each distillery visit revealing new insights.

Our search for the perfect partner continued, marked by weeks of exploration and discussions about the brand's name. After much deliberation, we chose "Señor Rio" as a tribute to my father and our family legacy. Señor Rio was my dad's nickname, which means Mr. River in English. It also stems from my maiden name, Rivera. We wanted to pay homage to him because, had I not reunited with him, there is no way I would be in the tequila business. Señor Rio is a tribute to my dad and gives our brand an identity. The decision resonated deeply with him, highlighting the convergence of past, present, and future in our tequila venture.

The family legacy is found in every aspect of our process and recipe. It starts with the farming of the plants on only one estate and keeping the agave plants in the earth for 8-12 years. We use nothing artificial; even the yeast comes from the honey of the plant. My father said this was passed down to him by his father and his grandfather.

Sharing our choice with my father brought immense joy and pride. Our tequila brand became more than a business—it became a heartfelt homage to family and destiny, intertwining the threads of our lives into a beautiful legacy.

"The Family Business" cocktail brings sweet and bold flavors that deliver complexity and a beautiful family vibe that comes from sweet memories and bold personalities.

# TEQUILA GODDESS

## INGREDIENTS

1 ½ oz. Blanco tequila
1 oz. Chareau aloe liqueur
1 oz. Cointreau
1 oz. fresh orange juice
1 oz. fresh lemon juice
2 oz. watermelon puree syrup

Add all ingredients into a Boston Shaker tin with ice and shake vigorously. Strain into an Alma double Old Fashioned glass. Garnish with a dehydrated lemon.

# SHARED PASSION

As we pursued information and contacts for getting our business off the ground, poor Jon fell victim to language nuances, showcasing the humor that can be found in making assumptions. We identified a distillery, La Cofradia, in Tequila, Mexico, that seemed like a strong possibility, so we planned a trip to visit their site. Jon's contact there was Rocio, and he had eagerly anticipated the opportunity to meet in person.

The encounter with Rocio took a delightfully unexpected twist as Jon was taken aback when he discovered the maestro of tequila correspondence was, in fact, a knowledgeable and beautiful woman—a true tequila goddess.

Guided by Rocio, we entered a picturesque distillery in Tequila, Mexico. The beautiful setting, surrounded by mountains and lush agave fields, felt like a dream. Mr. Carlos, the owner of La Cofradia distillery, embodied a blend of professionalism and a shared passion. The distillery's beauty was complemented by its staff, all of whom could have graced magazine covers.

Mr. Carlos's philosophy about hiring attractive office workers for daily interactions added a touch of Mexican charm. His willingness to recreate our family recipe and navigate regulatory approvals aligned perfectly with our aspirations.

Sipping tequila together, we toasted a partnership that felt blessed by personal connection and business-savvy. Leaving La Cofradia filled with a sense of accomplishment and camaraderie, Jon and I were ready for the next chapter in our tequila adventure—the journey marked by fate and family.

"Tequila Goddess" offers a fresh and vibrant flavor with added health benefits—a nod to the fates guiding us along the path to our dreams.

# Ingredients

2 oz. Añejo tequila

1 oz. Giffard vanilla liqueur

1 oz. Lillet Blanc

2 dashes chocolate bitters

2 dashes orange bitters

———————

Add all ingredients into a mixing glass with ice. Stir 8 times to the left and 8 times to the right. Strain into a rocks glass with large ice cube. Garnish with Luxardo cherry and smoke with a Flavor Blaster.

# OUR SUNDAY SANCTUARY

Every time we landed in Guadalajara, Mexico, its enchantment embraced us like a warm hug. Our trips to Guadalajara were to visit the distillery in Tequila, Mexico, where we produce Señor Rio tequila to check on the production and hand taste each batch.

The smooth customs process and the city's vibrant energy made our 2 ½-hour flight from Phoenix feel like a portal to our Mexican haven. Our home at the Rui, with its modern skyscraper design reminiscent of Manhattan, was our favorite. Its rooftop pool, lively bar, and live music set the perfect tone for our taste of Mexico. We strolled through the streets and discovered Lopez Mateo and Canelo's restaurant, which became our Sunday sanctuary. Arturo, the manager, treated us like old friends, creating a cozy atmosphere that felt like home. Waiters often mistook Jon for a TV personality, adding a touch of humor to our dining experiences. Jonathan's big gun sized arms from decades of weight lifting and full sleeves of tattoos caught their attention. The wait staff would whisper, "Look! Look at his arms," in Spanish and they wanted a picture with him as if he were Arnold Schwarzenegger. They would ask, smiling and a bit nervous, and they would jump at every chance to wait on our table just to see him. They thought he was Mr. Universe, which we would laugh about.

The culinary journey in Mexico was always a sensory feast.

Handmade tortillas, perfectly grilled meats, and unique delights like corn ice cream elevated every meal. Canelo's offered a haven where time slowed down. Jon enjoyed his cigar, Mariachis serenaded us, and the ambiance under the palapas with a man-made waterfall was pure relaxation. The antics of a parrot near the cascading waterfall also created memorable moments as we sipped tequila.

Mexico's strong family bonds were evident with playlands for children, showcasing the culture's emphasis on family unity. The celebration of life, love, and simple pleasures in Mexican culture humbled us. Each visit to Mexico was a testament to the magic found in its people and traditions.

The "Canelo's" is a Smoked Old Fashioned highlighting the smooth, cozy feeling we got from the retreats that became part of our frequent trips to Mexico.

# MAD HATTER

# INGREDIENTS

2 oz. Reposado tequila

2 oz. pamplemousse liqueur

1 oz. fresh lemon juice

1 oz. fresh orange juice

1 wild hibiscus flower with syrup

Add all ingredients into a Boston Shaker tin with ice and shake vigorously. Strain into rocks glass with a large ice cube. Garnish with a wild hibiscus flower with syrup.

# THE MAN IN THE HAT

The next phase as we forged ahead in creating Señor Rio Tequila's identity included designing our label and bottle.

We selected a vintage photo of my father wearing a distinctive hat to become our brand's inspiration. Jon called on a friend in New York to help with the design. He transformed the image and our vision into the logo that embodied my father's legacy. The label's color schemes were carefully chosen— silver, copper, and gold to represent the Blanco, Reposado, and Añejo varieties. Set against a striking black backdrop, this created a label that demanded attention.

Jon navigated the legal complexities of licensing and approvals required by the US Feds, Mexico, and State regulation boards to import alcohol. Meanwhile, I focused on the bottle's design. We envisioned an elegant decanter-like bottle and crafted a paper prototype, sleek and poised, reflecting our tequila's essence. Finding a domestic bottle manufacturer posed cost challenges until we discovered a US company outsourcing to China. There were initial setbacks with the cork. It did not have a tight seal and created leakage. Most brands use a natural cork, but we did not because cork breaks apart in liquid, so perfecting the synthetic cork to fit the bottle stem took some engineering. Despite those challenges our supplier's determination and patience yielded stunning sample bottles with elegantly baked labels.

The journey wasn't without hurdles. Each sample taught us valu-

# Señor Rio
## TEQUILA

able lessons. Patience was a major lesson for us. It was as if we were pregnant, forever waiting to birth this Señor Rio baby. In spite of that, our supplier's commitment and the promise of our distinctive tequila gracing shelves fueled our determination. Every obstacle reinforced our belief that Señor Rio Tequila would not only taste exquisite but also stand as a symbol of dedication and passion.

The "Mad Hatter" introduces citrus and hibiscus into an old favorite— the Tequila Sunrise—creating the excitement and intrigue that we encountered in this crucial time of shaping our identity as a tequila company.

White Lightning

## INGREDIENTS

2 oz. Blanco tequila

1 oz. Cointreau

1 oz. Orchard Pear liqueur

2 oz. lemon juice

3 oz. of canned pears

1 tsp. Chinese Five Spice

Add all ingredients into a Boston Shaker tin with ice and shake vigorously. Strain into a vampire wine glass with an ice cube. Garnish with a slice of pear and Chinese Five Spice sprinkled on top.

# HELLO, BEIJING

In a serendipitous turn, our supplier proposed a visit to China to see the manufacturing facility, marking our first time traveling in Beijing, post the 2008 Olympics. Jon's and my birthdays coincided with the journey, so we blended business with cultural immersion and culinary adventures.

Negotiating in bustling markets and showcasing my shopping prowess, our trip extended beyond business. The locals were immensely fascinated with Jon's physique and frequently requested photos of him.

Jon's taste for authentic Chinese cuisine led us to experience feasts complimenting diverse flavors, and we discovered the tradition of the "white lightning drink" (a.k.a. Chinese tequila), which added a spirited touch to our meals.

The factory tour revealed the intricacies of bottle crafting, culminating in our placing a significant order of 50,000 of our uniquely designed bottles and stoppers bearing the Señor Rio touch. Our time there also highlighted cultural nuances and economic realities, shedding light on the process of Chinese manufacturing and the dedication of workers. Witnessing their diligence and sacrifices underscored China's industrial strength and the human stories behind it.

Despite challenges, like resolving a cork issue with unconventional solutions, our stay in China left an enduring impression of cultural richness, culinary delights, and hardworking individuals shaping a dynamic landscape of tradition and progress.

The "White Lightening" blends the old world tradition of our tequila with this new world opening up to us through the signature tequila cocktail of a margarita and the addition of the infamous
Chinese five spice.

# Labor of Love

## Ingredients

1 oz. Reposado Tequila

¼ oz. Chambord

½ oz. peach puree

1 oz. fresh lemon juice

½ oz. Amaretto

Add all ingredients into a Boston Shaker tin with ice and shake vigorously. Strain into a coupe glass and garnish with a peach slice

# BORN ON CINCO DE MAYO

Returning to Arizona, Jon and I reveled in our progress. The tequila was maturing in Mexico, awaiting only the corks. However, the unveiling of sample corks revealed a major flaw. There was a significant issue with leakage.

Frustration mounted as our supplier struggled to solve the issue. With over $100,000 invested in 50,000 bottles and stoppers, the pressure was on.

Taking matters into our own hands, we sought a solution in Mexico City. We found a potential fix through a cork company called Tapones. They offered a two-piece synthetic rubber cork and plaster washer. The design was similar to how a plumber fixes a leak, and it offered hope.

Months of waiting followed as we navigated logistics and customs. The slow process tested our patience and added to our expenses, highlighting the complexities of international business.

Finally, the shipment arrived in Mexico, and we supervised the bottle filling at our tequila distillery on Cinco de Mayo 2009. Despite some assembly line challenges, we ensured the quality ourselves as part of our hands-on approach and commitment to Señor Rio's success.

As bottles were filled, cases sealed, and pallets stacked for shipping, Mr. Carlos joined us in toasting our perseverance and the future of Señor Rio. The journey, marked by setbacks and triumphs embodied our dedication and passion for crafting a tequila that represented more than just a business venture. It was a labor of love and commitment. It was the feeling of bringing our own child into the world.

The "Labor of Love" is a cocktail that captures the essence of love and textures. This sweet cocktail highlights the ingredients of a dessert crafted with love.

# What's in Your Briefcase

## 2 oz. Añejo tequila

Pour Tequila over two large cubes using the pour over coffee maker set. One ice cube on top and one ice cube in rocks glass.

# SHOWCASING

In May 2009, the first shipment arrived at our Gilbert, Arizona, warehouse. With determination, we began self-distributing the old-fashioned way. We carefully tucked three 750 ml tequila bottles in briefcases and hit the streets to cover more ground.

It was a blistering hot day when we started our mission to get Señor Rio directly into the hands of potential customers. We visited every establishment with a liquor license—from restaurants and bars to strip clubs and golf clubs—showcasing our beautiful bottles.

Years of experience in real estate gave me the confidence to approach potential clients, ask for the sale, and handle the various responses. Persistence and politeness were key. Any "No, not interested" translated to "Not now" in my selective hearing.

One memorable evening, we had a scheduled meeting at a high-end restaurant/bar. The manager asked us to wait at the bar, but as twenty minutes turned into an hour, our patience turned to frustration. Finally, I approached the manager and voiced our disappointment. His nonchalant demeanor solidified our decision to walk away.

During the following weekends, Jon and I dressed our best and went out to navigate the bustling bar scene. We hosted complimentary tastings and offered sips of our tequila. These events, although demanding, held potential success in each encounter.

Cinco de Mayo, the day Señor Rio was born, is a traditional Mexican celebration. We hosted tastings around this holiday to boost sales and establish our brand's presence. Although the pain in my feet mirrored the struggles I knew every cocktail server endured, it gave me newfound empathy for their daily grind.

Through the disrespect of some and the triumph of tastings, our journey wove a tale of resilience and an unyielding spirit that propelled us forward.

The "What's in Your Briefcase" cocktail showcases the Señor Rio spirit winners that we transported to establishments in our briefcases. The presentation and taste were crucial to our success. This is also showcasing a unique way of presenting tequila as they do in different parts of Mexico, typically in Sonora.

# HITTING THE STREETS

## INGREDIENTS

2 oz. Reposado tequila

1 oz. Carpano Antica Formulae vermouth

1 oz. Giffard grenadine

6 dashes of Fee Brothers fee foam

Add all ingredients into a Boston Shaker tin with ice and shake vigorously. Strain into a gold-rimmed coupe glass. Garnish with a red tuile wafer.

# AIN'T NO STOPPING US NOW

Selling tequila felt like traversing a desert of uncertainty, each bottle purchased offering a lifeline in our struggle. There were times when we had more tequila than dollars, but that only fueled our determination.

The Arizona summer heat pushed us northward. Sedona, with its breathtaking red rocks, became a frequent stop. Despite challenges, Arizona's liquor laws worked in our favor. Cash-and-carry allowed for immediate transactions. Jon and I grew closer as we journeyed north, placing our tequila in over 100 establishments throughout the valley, sometimes solo or as a duo sales team simply spreading our Tequila love.

Tastings and promotions became our forte. We wove Señor Rio into the fabric of these places. Each delivery and handshake was a building block for our brand. Road trips were about forging connections and leaving a mark on every establishment we visited.

"Ain't No Stopping Us Now" by McFadden and Whitehead became our theme song and energized our journey. To amplify our reach, we turned to Craigslist, hiring commission-based sales reps. One potential rep, JC, promised to sell "truckloads" but took another job the next day, teaching us a lesson in unpredictability. Hotel lobbies became our makeshift offices as we continued our grassroots approach, at times, recruiting family members to manage tastings.

In a market dominated by national brands, we aimed to disrupt the narrative with our top-shelf tequila and zero advertising dollars.

We finally experienced a breakthrough when Total Wine & More agreed to sell our brand. On our first delivery, we used shopping carts found in the parking lot. We didn't have a delivery truck lift to load our cases on their back loading dock. We delivered from our Senor Rio Jeep which the manager accepted by smiling and stating this an exception to the rule.

On the weekends, tastings at Total Wine became our stage to share our story and sample our tequila.

The support from customers turned each tasting into a celebration, signing bottles and sharing hugs with consumers who appreciated our artisanal quality. This response rein-

forced our decision for this personal touch. The joy we derived from seeing our bottles rung up at the checkout counter was a testament to our hard-earned success, as sweet as the smooth tequila we crafted.

"Hitting the Streets" addresses the determination we experienced in door-to-door sales, receiving orders and making those deliveries. This cocktail is refreshing and adds a mild vanilla sweetness from the vermouth complimenting the Reposado's cognac profile, embodying the sweet kindness of others.

Charity

# Ingredients

2 oz. Blanco tequila

1 oz. simple syrup

1 oz. fresh lemon juice

1 oz. pear puree

Add all ingredients into a Boston Shaker tin with ice and shake vigorously. Strain into an Alma 13 oz. clear highball glass with ice. Top with Fee Brothers Sparkling Mexican lime soda and garnish with a slice of pear.

# Giving Back

In the midst of our tequila journey, we embraced charity, turning our business into a platform for positive change. People approached us with hopes that Señor Rio would sponsor their charitable endeavors. They weren't reaching out to a faceless corporation; they were connecting with us, the heart and soul of Señor Rio.

Our website, senorrio.com, displayed not just our tequila but our personal involvement, including an email and phone number that went directly to us. This openness symbolized our genuine connection with the community.

Jon and I made a pact to support causes close to our hearts. At charity events, we shared not just our tequila but our personal story. Guests tasted our rich flavors and absorbed the essence of our journey, becoming participants in a cause that extended beyond the rim of their glasses.

We supported numerous charities, including Best Buddies, City of Hope, St. Jude Children's Research Hospital, The Boys and Girls Club, and many more. Each donation, tasting, and gift basket carried a piece of us and reflected our commitment to making a difference.

*A few highlights include:*

• Boris Diaw's All Star Charity Poker Tournament—Boris, an NBA professional athlete, welcomed us with open arms. Our Señor Rio bar found its place among celebrities, and Boris's personal gratitude made us feel like valued contributors.

• A Charity Event for Heart disease in Paradise Valley—we were invited by a master builder to a $20-million home, and our tequila tasting became a testament to the unexpected opportunities that arose from charity.

Despite being a small company, the warmth of appreciation from these organizations fueled our spirits. However, Jon informed me we were giving away more product than we were making in sales. Regrettably, our bottom line dictated that we had to decline some events; yet, we found solace in knowing we had made a difference. We also donated a portion of our sales to The Juvenile Diabetes Research Foundation, a cause close to our hearts due to Jonathan's father's death from diabetes.

Financial struggles were a harsh reality. It took five challenging years before we tasted profit. We lived frugally, tapping into savings and selling possessions to keep Señor Rio alive. The misconception that tequila owners lived lavishly was far from our truth. We sacrificed personal comfort to nurture our business.

In the tapestry of philanthropy, Señor Rio's imprint is one of compassion and shared humanity. We weren't just crafting tequila; we were crafting connections and leaving a lasting impact on the communities we touched.

The "Charity" cocktail offers something simple yet elegant, something that can be made by the dozen and served on a cocktail tray for a big ball room event. It features the Blanco tequila for the herbaceous notes, lemon for a light and refreshing note, and some pears to round off those flavors.

# BUILDING BLOCKS

## INGREDIENTS

1 oz. Reposado tequila

1 oz. La Pinta

2 oz. fresh orange juice

1 oz. Grand Marnier

Add all ingredients into a Boston Shaker tin with ice and shake vigorously. Strain into a Roly Double Old Fashioned Glass with a large ice cube. Garnish with Lego gummies.

# WE GOT A GIG

Seeking avenues beyond charity events to get exposure for our brand, we embraced opportunities to directly boost tequila sales. One standout venture was the Verde Canyon Tequila Sunset Train Ride in Clarkdale, Arizona. During the four-hour round trip drive there, we planned what we would speak about almost like a Sonny and Cher show. Together we taught tequila 101 to their passengers, complete with food pairings and cocktails, providing a captivating journey through the canyon. With no cell or internet connection, we enthralled our audience with stories, laughter, and tequila. The scenic backdrop transformed the train into an enter-tainment hub, creating new Señor Rio tequila enthusiasts.

The J.W. Marriott Star Pass in Tucson, Arizona, added another dimension to our outreach. Señor Rio tequila found a home at the Salud Bar in the resort. We hosted tequila classes on the terrace, elevating the experience. Again, the picturesque view provided a stage for immersive storytelling, and we eagerly shared our journey with the resort's guests. The classes, a fusion of education and relaxation paired with food, provided a unique opportunity for guests to savor the artistry behind Señor Rio tequila.

Once, J.W. Marriott hosted a tequila extravaganza, and the grounds became a sea of vendors. In an effort to stand out, we offered a Dead Sea salt and Blanco tequila scrub, providing hand massages and creating a sensation. The crowd loved it, and the good vibes flowed along with the tequila.

Señor Rio was sold in the gift shop of the Phoenician resort in Scottsdale, Arizona—the epitome of elegance—and was served in luxurious restaurants. Despite our polished exterior, we were hustling hard. Our story resonated with people—the

struggle behind the glitz was real. We looked like Tequila Kings, but reality was different.

Embarking on the rollercoaster journey of starting our own business and self-funding was a leap of faith. Jon meticulously counted every nickel while I remained the eternal optimist. Our lunch often consisted of peanut butter and jelly sandwiches as we hit the roads to promote our tequila. We knew we had something special with Señor Rio, so the sacrifices were an easy decision.

Though the struggle seemed unbearable at times, hearing from people about how much they loved supporting a small brand fueled our spirits. With genuine smiles, we'd share that we were just two love-birds with a passion for tequila. So, cheers to the days of peanut butter sandwiches, budget scrutiny, and unwavering belief—those were the building blocks of our tequila-fueled dream.

"Building Blocks" highlights the go-to tequila—Reposado—for building the foundation of a margarita but builds on it with citrus notes by incorporating fresh orange juice and a pomegranate liqueur for more layers of flavor. Being playful with our garnish and using gummy building blocks adds character to the cocktail.

El Señor the Mystic

# Ingredients

2 oz. Reposado tequila

1 oz. Grand Marnier

1 ½ oz. Real blackberry puree

2 dashes Fee Brothers orange bitters

1 oz. agave

1 oz. fresh lime juice

2 slices of jalapeño

Add all ingredients into a Boston Shaker tin with ice and shake vigorously. Strain into a Riedel Martini Glass. Garnish with a slice of fresh jalapeño.

# THE "B.S." MEETING

Finally, the time came for our grand adventure into the lion's den—the office of the largest distributor in Arizona. It all started with our persistent phone calls and a touch of arrogance on the other end, but we managed to secure a meeting with the VP after multiple attempts. Armed with enthusiasm, we waltzed into his colossal office, ready to make our mark. No time for small talk, we dove straight into the pitch. I could feel the nerves, but we laid it out: a dream partnership, Señor Rio gracing every establishment in Arizona and beyond.

The VP seemed impressed by the look of our bottles, claiming taste was secondary. But we insisted he give it a shot. Handing over our carefully crafted folder, we proudly declared Señor Rio as "pure elegance," our brand's tagline that we believed captured its essence. And then, the unexpected happened—the VP looked us square in the eyes and declared, "We are going to kick Patron's ass." Wait, what? Compete against Patron, the giant in the tequila realm? It was a moment that could either make us or break us. With a handshake that sealed our hopes, we left that office, hearts brimming with optimism.

Little did we know this meeting would soon turn into a cruel joke. Days turned into weeks, and weeks into an eternity of

silence. Our attempts to reconnect were met with an ominous void. No phone call, no
purchase order . . . just radio
silence. We were left in the
dark, grappling with uncertainty. Was the VP abducted
by aliens? Did he join a mon-
astery in the Himalayas? Our
minds concocted wild scenar-
ios, but the truth was lurking in
the shadows.

News broke, not through a
courtesy call, but via industry media. This distributor had
snatched the Patron account
from another distributor. We
finally reached him, expecting
answers. Instead, he dropped
the bomb: "Sorry, guys, we're
now Patron's distributor. No
room for Señor Rio. Good
luck!" Click.

And just like that, our dreams
were served a harsh dose of
reality. From the highs of "kick-
ing Patron's ass" to the icy
depths of rejection, it was a rollercoaster we never saw coming.
But we dusted off the disappointment, poured ourselves a
shot of resilience, and toasted
to the unpredictable journey of
the tequila trailblazers.

"El Señor the Mystic" showcases
a dance that many up-and-coming brands in the spirit industry endure every day around
the world. By introducing bold
flavors and a spicy finish with
blackberry and a kick of jala-
peños, this cocktail embodies
everything that Señor Rio represents.

# Wild West

## Ingredients

1 oz. Blanco tequila

1 oz. Cointreau

1 oz. fresh lime juice

½ oz. fresh lemon juice

¼ oz. cranberry juice

Dress the side of a rocks glass with fresh lime juice in a straight line and dust the glass with Tajin Clasico with lime mild seasoning mix. Add all ingredients into a Boston Shaker tin with ice and shake vigorously. Strain into a rocks glass with a large ice cube.

# THE DISTRIBUTOR DANCE

The tumultuous dance we faced with distributors took us from the highs of anticipation to the lows of disappointment. After our Patron-sized heartbreak, finding a distributor became our holy grail. We yearned for someone to handle the sales and deliveries, freeing us to weave the tapestry of Señor Rio's brand story through tastings and events.

Enter a seasoned industry veteran, a man with forty years in the field under his belt. He showed interest when we shared our list of over 100 accounts, a feat that earned a knowing nod. "Not easy," he remarked, and we couldn't agree more. The deal was on the table. He'd consider taking our product, but he wanted our contact list. A fair exchange, we thought, as we eagerly handed over the keys to our sales kingdom.

A few days later, the call came. They were ready to place an order, a modest beginning with just a few pallets. Victory dance time! The distributor's sales team was next on our agenda. We painted the canvas of Señor Rio's essence, and they seemed genuinely intrigued, sampling with courtesy and curiosity. We even offered to ride shotgun with the reps, introducing Señor Rio to their accounts and boosting sales.

Back in the trenches, we tirelessly hosted tastings and events every weekend, pouring our passion into every drop of tequila. Social media and website updates became our allies in the quest for a devoted following. As distribution unfurled its wings in Arizona, we set our sights on other states.

Cue the Texas distributor. His initial burst of praise for our product and presentation was music to our ears. But then, the discordant note struck: he needed marketing dollars, a cool million to be precise, to make us millionaires. Politely declining, we hung up, realizing that our path to tequila glory wasn't paved with seven-digit investments.

Undeterred, we continued the distributor courtship, targeting smaller players who might appreciate the charm of our boutique brand. The "big boys," as we affectionately called them, were busy peddling the national giants with deep pockets for marketing. Some dropped a staggering $85 million annually on advertising while we clung to our dreams with nothing but determination and a prayer.

In this wild tequila rodeo, we were the underdogs, armed with passion, grit, and maybe just a hint of craziness. But, hey, who needs a million dollars when you've got the spirit of Señor Rio in every bottle and the sheer audacity to take on the giants? We stayed focused on the journey, the struggle, and the hope that one day our tequila tale would echo across every bar in the land.

"Wild West" highlights the bittersweet journey to find a distributor by incorporating the sweetness of Cointreau and the tartness of cranberry. But the combination won't leave you feeling bitter.

La Biblioteca

## Ingredients

1 oz. Reposado tequila
1 oz. apple juice
1 oz. fresh lime juice
1 oz. local honey syrup
1 oz. Real apple puree syrup
2 dashes of Hella chili bitters

Add all ingredients into a Boston Shaker tin with ice and shake vigorously. Strain into a rocks glass with a large ice cube. Garnish with a slice of apple.

# NO LIBRARY CARD NEEDED

Ah, the windy streets of Chicago, where the cold bites to the bone and the winters are a force to be reckoned with. After the Arizona distributor's recommendation, we found ourselves in Illinois at the first of the year, attempting to conquer the formidable market. The Illinois distributor threw down the gauntlet: convince Binny's—the largest retail liquor store in Illinois—and the distribution deal would be ours.

So, we met with the buyer at Binny's, armed with our tequila charm and a tale to tell. The buyer liked what he tasted, nodded at our story, and gave us the classic "I'll be in touch." Lo and behold, the next day, the Illinois distributor called, announcing that Binny's was placing an order—a $20,000 purchase order, to be precise. Hooray! A sweet victory.

Eager to expand our empire, we turned to Craigslist to assemble a legion of Señor Rio representatives. We conducted phone interviews and hired a handful of candidates without laying eyes on them. Back in the chilly embrace of Chicago, we unloaded a truckful of supplies for our new recruits. But waiting at the curb for them in the piercing cold of January felt like a punishment akin to a frozen dog in the backyard.

With a car packed to the brim, we embarked on a journey of training sessions and meetings. The Harold Washington Public Library, our makeshift office, served us well, especially with its irresistible price tag: free.

Our new reps were enthusiastic, embracing the startup spirit. The distributor was impressed that we had a sales crew hitting the streets, ready to conquer the liquor world. Tastings at Binny's warmed up the customers, and sales ensued despite the bone-chilling weather.

But as we wrapped up our Illinois mission, the yearning for Arizona's warmth intensified. I may have endured Chicago winters for decades, but now the cold was an unwelcome guest. Jonathan, while a New Yorker by origin, shared my sentiment. Living in Arizona as long as I have, my blood has thinned now, and I even get chilly at the supermarket in the frozen food section, which feels like an arctic tundra. Arizona's daily sunshine became our beacon.

The hired reps did make sales and stuck around for about a year. We even returned for ride-a-longs with the distributor's sales team, but the pace was sluggish as we only saw another modest $8,000 purchase order trickle in. We persisted with tastings to boost our brand, but the distributor eventually fell out of sync. Despite our efforts, we learned the hard truth of the alcohol business: without marketing dollars, even a promising tequila can be left on the shelf. And so, with a mix of lessons learned and a bit of disappointment, our journey through the frosty streets of Chicago came to an end. Onward we marched, ready for the next twist in our tequila saga.

"La Biblioteca" (Library) reflects the sweet reception we received in Chicago countered with the longing to be back in the warm embrace of Arizona by introducing some honey for a sweet component and apples to give you that big city vibe but punched up with a hint of spice.

# SCARS EARNED

## INGREDIENTS

2 oz. Blanco tequila

1 oz. Cointreau

1 oz. St. Germain

4 fresh raspberries, muddled

2 jalapeño slices

Add all ingredients into a Boston Shaker tin with ice and shake vigorously. Strain into a vintage goblet/wine glass with a large ice cube. Garnish with four fresh raspberries on a gold cocktail pick.

# LESSONS LEARNED

California beckoned and, armed with industry magazine ads, we dove into the sea of small distributors. One seemed promising—a family-run business with a long history. We struck a deal, a consignment agreement that sent shivers down our entrepreneurial spines where we were to front $20,000 in product. Months passed and the promised payment remained elusive. Calls went unanswered, and suspicion lingered. We hatched a gangster-style plan: rent a truck, stake out the warehouse, and reclaim our tequila case by case. We lost about $5,000 in the process, but at least we escaped the clutches of this unscrupulous distributor.

Next on the journey was Connecticut where we cautiously entered into an exclusive agreement with a small distributor. The initial excitement dimmed as the orders rolled in. They repeatedly demanded more free product and that we foot the bill for freight. Tensions rose when we requested payment for freight, leading to the cancellation of an order. The struggle intensified, and we decided to end the relationship. But Connecticut liquor laws resulted in a convoluted process involving claims, hearings, and certified mail. The creep of all creeps demanded payment for release, and we stood firm, refusing to be bullied.

Three long years later, the nightmare concluded. We booked flights, reserved hotel rooms, and prepared to face the creep in court. However, in a surprising twist, the hearing was canceled and the release was signed. The ordeal was over, and we were free from the clutches of the distributor from hell.

Lessons learned, scars earned, we emerged stronger and wiser. The journey through the liquor industry's wild west taught us that not all distributors are allies, and some battles are fought in boardrooms and courtrooms. The intricacies of the liquor business continued to weave a complex tale, where distributors wield the power to either elevate a brand or plunge it into obscurity.

As we breathed a sigh of relief, we looked forward to brighter days and a smoother sip of success on the tequila trail.

The "Scars Earned" cocktail focuses on the flowers you smell as you get up off the mat after getting knocked down in battle, and muddled raspberries reflect the bruises you take away from that fight.

# Salud, Jimmy

## Ingredients

1 oz. Añejo tequila

1 oz. Dry Curaco

1 oz. Giffard Creme Peach de Vigne

1 oz. fresh lemon juice

A pinch of cinnamon

Add all ingredients into a Boston Shaker tin with ice and shake vigorously. Strain into a gold-rimmed coupe glass. Garnish with a slice of peach.

# SOUTHERN CHARM

Despite past woes, we sent our bottles of liquid joy and product sheets to various out-of-state companies. In the unpredictable world of distribution, we found ourselves cautiously optimistic with a Tennessee distributor. After waiting and persistent follow-ups, the Tennessee distributor gave us a resounding "yes."

Eager and determined, we flew out to meet them. They started with a small order and proposed we join their sales reps to introduce our brand. We eagerly hit the streets, one establishment at a time, embracing Southern charm as sales reps guided us through the Tennessee market. Orders rolled in, and we enjoyed the warmth of Southern hospitality.

However, as quickly as the orders arrived, they dwindled. The initial excitement gave way to familiar frustration: "out of sight, out of mind." Just when we needed a boost, we learned that Tennessee celebrity Jimmy Van Zant had fallen in love with our tequila. Grateful, we planned a trip to express our thanks.

We met Jimmy and his wife Zoe, who welcomed us into their home with genuine warmth. Over dinner, we bonded, and in a spontaneous gesture, we had Jimmy sign a guitar we bought earlier that day. The day was filled with chili, music, and laughter, forging a true friendship. The guitar still hangs in our office as a poignant reminder of a friendship built on tequila, music, and Southern spirit. Though Jimmy has passed, his memory and Southern charm live on in our hearts.

Our distribution journey continued with a Georgia distributor. Initial meetings were promising, and a small order was placed. We joined forces with sales reps, promoting our brand with determination.

However, history seemed to repeat itself. The refrain "out of sight, out of mind" rang out, and frustration grew as our brand was overshadowed by larger, financially backed national brands. The industry's preference for well-funded giants became clear, leaving our passionate, up-and-coming brand struggling for attention.

Despite the financial constraints, we pressed on, determined to carve our path. We questioned why the industry favored big brands over passionate startups, but we remained hopeful that perseverance and a bit of luck might tilt the scales in our favor. Here's to hoping our story—the remarkable journey of an underdog in the competitive world of distribution—becomes one for the books.

"Salud, Jimmy" is a toast to our friend who embraced us and our tequila with an open heart. We raise our glass to many more nights in his spirit. Peaches come to mind when I think of the South, and Jimmy embodied Southern hospitality, so that is the dominant note in this cocktail.

# The Pursuit of Happiness

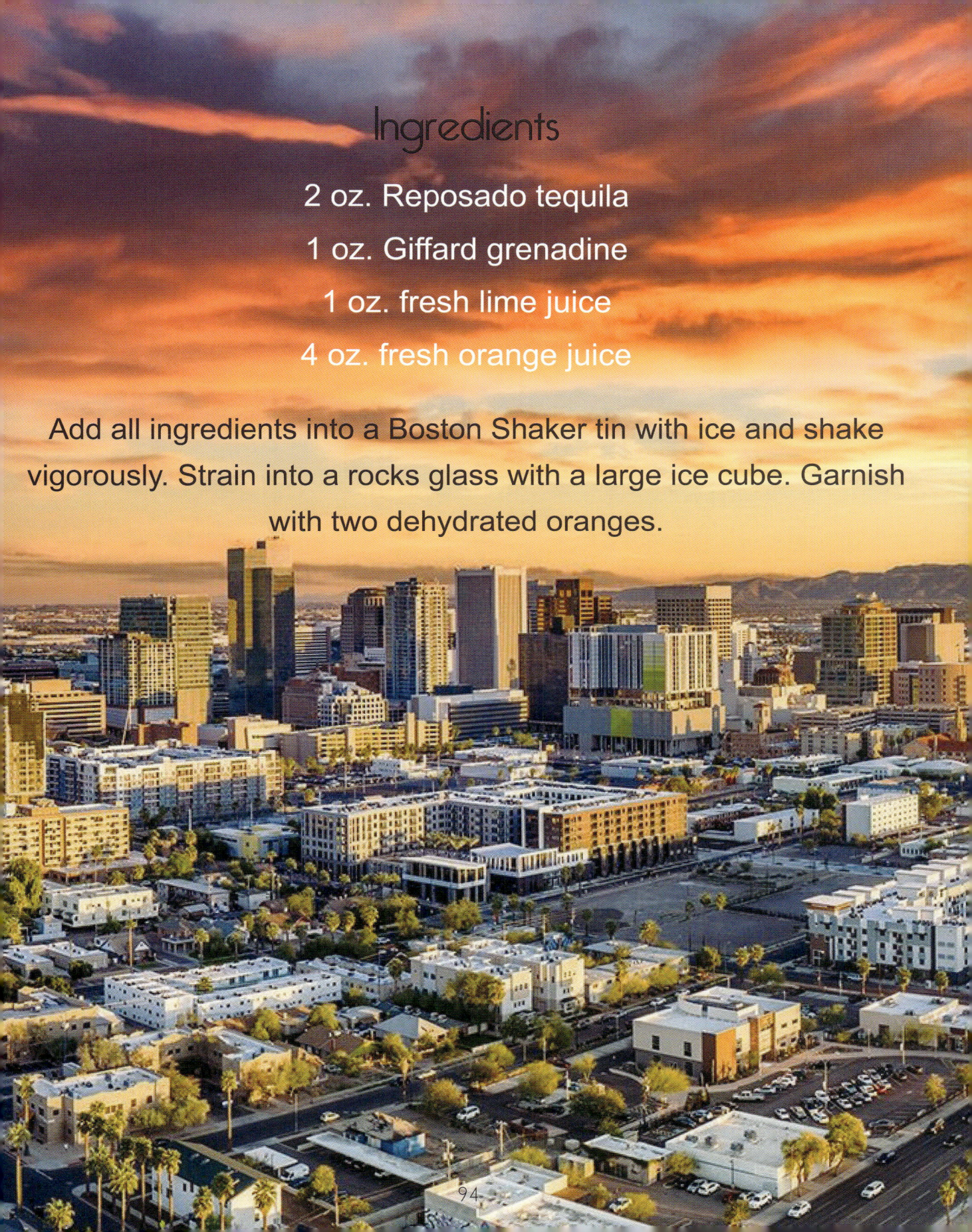

## Ingredients

2 oz. Reposado tequila

1 oz. Giffard grenadine

1 oz. fresh lime juice

4 oz. fresh orange juice

Add all ingredients into a Boston Shaker tin with ice and shake vigorously. Strain into a rocks glass with a large ice cube. Garnish with two dehydrated oranges.

# ONWARD

In the heart of our home state, Arizona, dissatisfaction with our current distributor for Señor Rio spurred a decision. It was time to find a partner who would wholeheartedly embrace our brand and propel it to new heights. With determination in our steps, Jon and I sought out another distributor, one that would be the perfect fit.

Walking into the office of the potential distributor, located amidst their bustling warehouse, we exuded confidence. The owner welcomed us, intrigued by the prospect of tasting our tequila. As he called in his assistant, we poured each type with anticipation, watching them swirl, sniff, and sip. The verdict was music to our ears. The taste was exceptional, the smoothness palpable, the bottle beautiful, and our story heartfelt. The distributor expressed his honor in selling our brand, sealing the deal with a firm handshake.

With an immediate request for our account list and an order placed, it felt like a fresh start. A presentation for the distributor's team was on the horizon. This smaller, more engaged group showed genuine interest and excitement for Señor Rio, leaving us optimistic that we had finally found the distributor that aligned with our vision.

As we geared up for the ride-alongs, the distributor surprised us by suggesting that we introduce them to our accounts first. It seemed like a prudent move, ensuring a smoother transition and avoiding the pitfalls of losing accounts. We embarked as they reciprocated on joint visits, introducing our brand to their accounts.

The synergy felt right, and orders kept flowing in. We were hopeful and optimistic, seeing a promising future ahead. However, in less than a year, the harsh reality surfaced. The distributor had other plans for our accounts, steering them toward different brands. Once again, we found ourselves at a crossroads, realizing this partnership was not going to be mutually beneficial and we had to part ways.

Our journey continued, marked by resilience and the unwavering belief that the right distributor was out there, ready to champion our brand. As we faced the disappointment with grace, we braced ourselves for the next chapter in the pursuit of the perfect match. We pressed onward, always with an eye on the horizon, knowing that the right partner was just around the corner.

"Pursuit of Happiness" represents the hope we held for happier days to come. The flavors capture the fruit of our labors that we knew were on the horizon.

# Where's the Love?

## Ingredients

1 oz. Reposado tequila

1 oz. fresh lemon juice

1 oz. Real guava puree

Add all ingredients into a Boston Shaker tin with ice and shake vigorously. Strain into a rocks glass with a large ice cube. Top with Fever Tree sparking yuzu. Garnish with a blue tuile cookie.

# LOOKING FOR THE PERFECT MATCH

Jonathan and I eagerly pursued a large distributor in Arizona, bombarding them with calls and emails until the vice president, weary of our persistence, agreed to meet. Excited, we arrived early for the meeting only to learn from the receptionist that the vice president was off that day. We had shown up a month early. Embarrassed but amused, we apologized and left, resolving to return at the right time.

A month later, we met the vice president who was impressed by our tequila and the awards it had garnered. He admitted he only gave us a chance because he knew we wouldn't give up, but he was glad we kept at it. With that, we had secured a new distributor in Arizona.

Our first order, a promising pallet, marked a new chapter. We offered to support the distributor by introducing Señor Rio and educating their sales team on our product. We were invited to present at a monthly meeting with over 100 attendees. While we encountered technical difficulties when our power point presentation didn't work on their screen we still pressed on and shared our story.

However, the relationship didn't meet expectations. The distributor lost accounts, gave minimal brand push, and preferred national brands with deep pockets. Even when restaurants wanted more Señor Rio, the distributor's sales reps were indifferent.

Discovering some distributors had a practice of burying a brand or giving it away as a free product, we knew it was time to pivot. We resumed the search for a distributor who would champion our brand with passion.

In the world of distribution, the journey is full of twists and turns. Yet, with resilience and determination, we pressed on, ever hopeful that the right partner was out there, ready to embrace Señor Rio and help it flourish. The pursuit continued, fueled by the belief that there was a perfect match out there.

"Where Is the Love?" is full of love, merging fruits and sparkling sodas with this special tequila to reflect our pursuit of a partner who would hold the same passion for Señor Rio that we do.

# SHANGHAI NIGHTS

## INGREDIENTS

1 oz. Blanco tequila
1 oz. Dry Curaçao
2 oz. fresh lemon juice
½ oz. Giffard grenadine
¼ oz. Giffard anise
½ oz. cranberry juice

Add all ingredients into a Boston Shaker tin with ice and shake vigorously. Strain into a rocks glass with large ice cube. Garnish with two dehydrated lemons.

# A HOLE IN THE GROUND

Our journey to find the right suppliers led us back to China, specifically for bottle stoppers, since our Mexican glass factory could not produce them. We contacted a broker named Stanley who impressed us with his English and promises. Despite the time difference, we engaged in late-night calls and wired funds for the molds. The samples exceeded our expectations, marking the start of a positive relationship.

We ordered bottles and stoppers as needed with shipments delivered to our distillery in Tequila, Mexico, and the cork company in Mexico City for assembly. Managing logistics across continents required con-stant communication, often late at night, which I enjoyed doing in my pajamas.

After two years, we decided to meet Stanley in person. We planned a trip to Shanghai, enduring a 16-hour flight from Phoenix. We met Stanley and discussed our partnership over a grand lunch. We tried many different dishes like elephant ear-sized mushrooms and lots of noodles with minced meat and veggies. Jon suddenly had to run to the bathroom and, after he was gone for a while, I went to check on him. As I waited outside the men's room I heard some laughter. I managed to peek in and saw the bathroom attendant chuckling as he tried to help Jon. It appeared that he had a bad case of the runs and had stripped down to his birthday suit to avoid making a mess on his clothing. I stepped in and offered to give him a hand. He was a bit embarrassed but found humor in this situation. For those of you who don't know, the bathroom stalls in China are primitive with no toilet, no seat, just a hole in the ground. When nature calls you answer like a bear in the woods. Luckily, he emerged victorious from this bathroom escapade and passed on eating more.

Next on the list was a visit to a box supplier, which turned into a linguistic adventure with some initial confusion leading to the presentation of cereal boxes. Patience prevailed, and we eventually reached an agreement for sample boxes. We also visited a glass factory showroom to discuss design ideas requiring meticulous explanations for our second-generation extra Añejo bottle

Stanley equipped me with basic Mandarin phrases to help me navigate the local markets in Jinan. Once our business was completed, we still managed to pack memorable moments into our brief stay in Shanghai. We strolled along the Bund, visited an underground market where Jon got custom sports jackets, and we enjoyed live jazz at the Long Bar of the Waldorf Astoria. I can't forget The French Concession area with its European charm; it left a lasting impression.

This international business journey taught us the importance of diligence, communication, and adaptability. Despite the challenges, we continued our quest for the right partners, ever hopeful for future success.

"Shangai Nights" pays homage to the traditional Shanghai Night cocktail but with a Señor Rio twist.

# The
# Situationship

# Ingredients

1 oz. Añejo tequila

½ oz. Blue Curaçao

½ oz. Clement Rum coconut liqueur

1 oz. fresh lime juice

¼ oz. Real pineapple puree

Add all ingredients into a Boston Shaker tin with ice and shake vigorously. Strain into a gold-rimmed coupe glass. Garnish with a red heart tuile.

# IN THE NICK OF TIME

After five years of navigating the labyrinth of liquor distribution, facing one uphill battle after another, we found ourselves exhausted by the whirlwind of struggle yet still determined to succeed.

And then, as if the universe decided it was time for a turning point, the phone rang. It was Total Wine & More, an organization synonymous with excellence in the realm of alcohol retail. Known as America's wine, beer, and spirits superstore, they boasted an impressive selection of over 8,000 wines, 3,000 spirits, and 2,500 beers, all offered at the best prices. The family-owned venture founded by brothers David and Robert Trone over twenty-five years ago had grown into a 3-billion-dollar empire with over 200 stores in twenty-four states.

But what struck a chord with us beyond their business acumen was their philanthropic endeavors, contributing millions to charities. David Trone recommended the book Give and Take: Why Helping Others Drives Our Success by Adam Grant, which highlighted their values.

Señor Rio was sold only at their Arizona stores as it was an account we opened a few years back locally. We had submitted our tequila for their Spirits Direct program—an exclusive agreement where they would carry our tequila brand in all of their stores nationwide that were permitted by state laws through various distributors. This was a game-changer. They focused on being a store within a store to have products that no other store carried. This partnership was made for small producers, exactly what we were with Señor Rio. Despite the request to reduce our pricing, which we obliged, the first order for about 1,000 cases was a lifeline.

Months earlier, Jon had invested the proceeds from selling his first house into our company—a leap of faith that now seemed serendipitous. As we faced the need for more resources to keep our dream afloat, the question arose: whose house would be the next sacrifice? In this tender moment, a decision unfolded. Jon graciously chose to merge his world with mine and relinquish his current home. I, a mother of two daughters and guardian of two furry companions, opened my home to him.

With the practicality of life's challenges, my real estate license became a beacon of hope. Jon's impeccably maintained house (a reflection of his character) found a new owner almost instantly. The proceeds from this sale became the infusion of capital that breathed life into our shared dream. His investment, both financial and emotional, became the cornerstone that saved our company from the brink. And the chapters of our story intertwined further as cohabitation became our new reality. Days turned into nights, and every moment was an exquisite fusion of shared dreams and shared spaces.

He was not just a business partner, but a companion who made every night an exploration of the heart. In the quiet moments and the shared laughter, we discovered a depth of understanding that went beyond words.

Total Wine became our guardian angel, propelling us toward financial stability. We concentrated on tastings at Total Wine stores, averaging over 100 a year, and then traveling to various states when we could afford it. Grateful doesn't begin to describe our emotions. The managers and team members welcomed us with open arms, and soon, it felt like we were part of the Total Wine family.

To this day, I am filled with gratitude for Total Wine & More. Their support by believing in and embracing our company transformed it. When I share our story during tastings, the customers wish us continued success, and I give out more hugs than bottles sold. Being a Spirits Direct partner symbolizes a deep connection that we have formed with this exceptional organization. Some blessings do arrive in the nick of time, and, for us, Total Wine was that blessing.

"Situationship" embodies the unique and complex nature of relationships in today's world, offering unique flavors you typically would not find together, but they work!

# ONE FOR THE ROAD

## Ingredients

1/2 oz. Blanco Tequila

1 oz. Real peach puree

4 oz. Prosecco

Add all ingredients except Prosecco into a Boston Shaker tin with ice and shake vigorously. Strain the first two ingredients into a bird-shaped cocktail glass. Finish with Prosecco and garnish with sprigs of rosemary and one edible flower.

# ON THE ROAD AGAIN

Who knew the glamorous life of tequila entrepreneurs would include Expedia deals, improvised bug spray, and the occasional rendezvous with truckers and hookers? Jon and I became masters of the art of budget travel, monitoring airfares, hotel rates, and rental car packages like it was our own reality TV show. Living out of a suitcase became our modus operandi, and we embraced it with all the grace of seasoned wanderers.

Our partnership with Total Wine & More was a godsend, placing us in over 200 stores nationwide. This became our routine: fly in, pick up the rental car, check into the hotel, eat, sleep, and host in-store tequila tastings, sometimes two a day. Budget constraints dictated our choices early on, leading us to those charming fly-by-night hotels where you had to park your own car, carry your own luggage, and climb an outside staircase to your room.

I recall one memorable night when I discovered a sink crawling with black ants. In a moment of panic, I grabbed my hairspray, turning it into makeshift bug spray. That incident marked the birth of our innovative skills, and bug spray quickly found its place on our packing list.

As we navigated the world of budget lodging, we stayed in places with loud drunks, outdated furniture, and occasionally those annoying mildew smells. TripAdvisor and other review sites became our trusty guides, though sometimes they led us astray. Eventually, we upgraded to Holiday Inn and the occasional hotel with a happy hour (a sign that we were "moving on up").

Dining was our indulgence, and we splurged on breakfasts and even a few happy hours. Our interactions with customers and store teams became integral to our success. Sometimes, Jon and I hosted tastings together, bringing a dynamic duo vibe once again that was part Sonny and Cher, while conducting a Tequila 101 class.

Our tastings, documented on social media, displayed happy tequila smiles, and we joked that when taking the Señor Rio tequila flight (sampling all three expressions of tequila) you could keep your shoes on and didn't need a boarding pass. The tequila flight became our signature, and we'd explain the nuances of each expression of Señor Rio—the Blanco, Reposado, and Añejo—making it Tequila 101 at our table.

I may not have been a young, sexy promo girl; but, as the co-founder of our company, I shared our story with pride. Customers were receptive, and some were so impressed that they asked us to sign their purchased bottles. It became a habit, and later, we decided to offer to sign each bottle, turning them into collectibles.

When Jon humorously mentioned that his signature was worth five bucks and could get you a Starbucks coffee, people loved it. We were just being ourselves, and what you saw was what you got. I would share with a smile that one day in my 80s, I would stumble upon our bottle in an antique shop, and that is when I would know we had truly made it.

"One for the Road" represents our life on the road as free birds with its unique glass and the sparkle of the Prosecco that injects vibrance and vitality, just as our connections with customers gave us.

Señor Rio is *Love* in a bottle.

DREAMS

## INGREDIENTS

1 oz. Reposado tequila

1 oz. Cointreau orange liqueur

1 oz. fresh lemon juice

1 oz. Real kiwi puree

Dress a Nick and Nora glass with fresh lime juice on the rim and dust Tajin mild lime seasoning mix. Add all ingredients into a Boston Shaker tin with ice and shake vigorously. Strain into the glass. Garnish with edible coral tuile.

# THE DESERT ANGELS

We were filled with excitement, nerves, and a dash of desperation. We had gone as far as we could on our own resources and needed backers. We found a group of potential saviors in the Desert Angels (think Shark Tank but on a smaller scale), and after submitting our startup for consideration, we got the golden ticket: a chance to present our case.

Now, envision a night in a cheap hotel near the freeway, a symphony of traffic noises creating a soundtrack. I barely slept, tossing, and turning with the concerns, anticipation, and preparations rolling through my head. We were determined to nail our presentation, so we rehearsed like a pair of over-zealous actors preparing for the performance of a lifetime.

The day arrived, and with bags under our eyes, we entered the room, trying to mask our nervous excitement. We had about twenty minutes to dazzle the Desert Angels with our brilliance . . . or at least make them believe we knew what we were doing. Jon and I explained the liquor industry intricacies, how tequila was the rising star, and how we were carving our niche one bottle at a time through grassroots marketing. They seemed impressed, intrigued even.

But then came the ominous questions. Jon, in his finest conservative financial projection fashion, did a stellar job answering and alleviating their concerns. Confidence filled the room and, for a moment, we felt we were on the verge of securing the investment we so desperately sought.

Alas, the punchline was delivered—they wouldn't invest because of our lack of experience in the liquor industry. Despite our passion, the fact that Jon had a stint in a liquor store during his college days, and my sales background in real estate, it didn't quite cut it for them.

We left that room disappointed but undeterred. As we trudged out, heads held high, though dreams momentarily crushed, we muttered to ourselves, "We'll show them. One day they'll regret passing up on this tequila-fueled brilliance." And so, the saga continued with the rollercoaster of hope, humor, and an unyielding belief that our day would come, with or without the Desert Angels.

"Dreams" is a cocktail embodying the ups and downs that are an inevitable part of pursuing your passions. The delicate tuile represents the heartbreaks of our experience. The spice that fueled us is carried through with the Tajin seasoning. And the kiwi, with its fuzzy skin, conveys the blurry vision of success still before us that we knew was out there even if the path wasn't clear.

# SHOW READY

## INGREDIENTS

1 oz. Blanco tequila

1 oz. melon liquor

1 oz. fresh lemon juice

1 oz. watermelon puree

8 dashes of Fee Brothers Fee Foam

Add all ingredients into a Boston Shaker tin with ice and shake vigorously. Strain into classic crystal goblet. Garnish with dehydrated lemons.

# NEWS-WORTHY

Our first warehouse had all the charm of a haunted house minus the ghosts but with a surplus of empty bottles of tequila. Office furniture was an expendable convenience when our budget was exclusively dedicated to creating liquid gold. We were the masters of resource allocation, and our workspace reflected it . . . rather, the lack thereof.

Then came the unexpected call from a local cable station interested in featuring us on a show called "Su Vida," meaning "His Life" in Spanish. Perfect! A chance to showcase our passion, our story, and our almost non-existent office. But before we could say "¡Tequila!," we had to scramble and find furniture with our whopping budget of $200.

Craigslist and IKEA became our office makeover partners. The reception desk, unfortunately, took a tumble during delivery, but never fear! Jon's handy friend Razz swooped in like a tequila superhero to save the day and made it functional. With a week to go, our office went from a desolate wasteland to a place that almost resembled professionalism.

The day of the show arrived, and with my daughter playing the role of receptionist, Jon and I suited up. We were as professional as two tequila enthusiasts could be. Nervously, we spilled our story and passion to the cameras, and the show

aired a week later. Much to our dismay, we never got a sneak peek, but the piece looked good, and we received a few phone calls from friends who had caught the show.

"Show-Ready" brings in watermelon for a smooth taste on the mouth. Then, the cocktail is elevated with Fee Foam to create a magical texture, representing the magic we pulled off in setting a presentable stage for our TV debut.

# Don't Judge

## Ingredients

1 oz. Blanco tequila

1 oz. Añejo tequila

1 oz. St. Germain elderflower liqueur

2 oz. sweet and sour mix

1 oz. agave syrup

4 muddled cucumbers

2 slices of jalapeño

Add all ingredients into a Boston Shaker tin with ice and shake vigorously. Strain into a cocktail rocks glass with a large ice cube. Garnish with a cucumber peel rolled into a flower held together by a gold cocktail pick in the center.

# TEQUILA OLYMPIAN

In the thrilling quest for recognition, Jon and I decided to throw our tequila into the ring of industry competitions. We were ready to battle, armed with our liquid gold and a dream. The first contender on our list was the Los Angeles International Spirits Competition. We decided to focus on the packaging category. After all, presentation is key, right?

We were elated to receive the bronze medal and felt like tequila Olympians, proudly hanging that medal as a declaration of our triumph. Compared to entries from all around the world, our bottle stood out.

The taste of Mexico Spirits Festival and Competition beckoned next. This time, we journeyed to San Diego, California, for the event. The entry fee was manageable, but setting up a tasting table or paying for sponsorship was a financial acrobatic feat we couldn't quite master. As our bottle joined the ranks of hundreds on display, we reveled in the experience.

However, the aftertaste of disappointment lingered. After the dinner ceremony, we discovered that our bottle had vanished—a real-life tequila heist. It turned out someone had pinched it, leaving us both perplexed and somewhat flattered. We did manage to secure a bronze medal for our Blanco tequila, but it was a small consolation.

The next day we stopped at a liquor store that sold our brand. We were letting customers know about our new accolades, and the owner happened to overhear us. He introduced himself and said he was one of the blind-tasting judges. He spilled the tequila beans that the competition organizers had their version of a private tequila summit, and the winners were handpicked behind closed doors. It seemed our hunch about paid sponsorships was spot on.

Unwavering in our determination, we set our sights on the grand stage—the San Francisco World Spirits Competition, the heavyweight champion of the spirits world. No biased sponsorships or shady dealings here; it was all about the taste. The blind tasting took four days, and our entries faced judgment without any producer or price bias.

Cue the drumroll! Our Señor Rio Añejo tequila and Señor Rio Cafe Elegancia both snagged gold medals, reaching the pinnacle of spirit achievement. Señor Rio Reposado tequila proudly wore the bronze. Meanwhile, Señor Rio Blanco and Señor Rio Extra Añejo earned silver medals for their refinement and complexity.

These awards were not just shiny additions to our collection; they were universal endorsements of our brand's quality. With each medal, we whispered to consumers, "It isn't just us saying it; these awards speak louder than we ever could." The recognition set us apart from the sea of competitors, and we basked in the glow of our liquid triumphs.

"Don't Judge" evokes the rewarding moments as well as the disappointments in pursuing accolades for our hard work. The floral notes of this margarita combined with a little kick in a unique vessel, showcases both the refreshing taste of recognition and the bite of rejection.

*Pure Elegance in a Bottle*

LIMITED EDITION

LIMITED EDITION

## Ingredients

1 oz. Reposado tequila
1 oz. Lillet Rose
1 oz. Orchard Pear brandy & cognac
½ oz. Pataka cucumber liqueur
1 oz. fresh lemon juice

Dress a Riedel double rocks glass with a cucumber peel and a large ice cube. Stamp the large ice cube first with a star or letter "S" before pouring in the cocktail. Add all ingredients into a Boston Shaker tin with ice and shake vigorously. Strain into the prepared glass.

# *Warehouse Nightmare*

As we outgrew our small warehouse and needed a new home for our tequila, we sought a new location, and a must-have was a loading dock. Our current warehouse was a nightmare when it came time for pickups, turning the task into an all-day siesta because the trucking guys decided to play hide and seek with their schedules. And poor Jon, bless his tequila-loving soul, had to shrink-wrap pallet after pallet in sauna-like conditions, risking a dizzy spell or two.

The real kicker was that with no dock we'd watch trucks roll in with no lift and no easy loading in sight. Our hearts would sink faster than a shot of bad tequila. Eventually, a forklift rental came to the rescue, but loading the pallets in the narrow alley was nerve-wracking.

But, if you haven't noticed by now, we're not quitters! We honored that lease like it was a sacred tequila ritual until we decided enough was enough and embarked on a quest for the warehouse of our dreams. Enter the public warehouse, our knight in shining shrink wrap! They had it all—shrink wrapping, docks, forklifts, and actual reliable schedules. It was like trading a donkey for a Ferrari. Or so we thought.

Turns out, even the fanciest warehouses can have a few skeletons in their closets.

One day, we got a call from Real Estate Drama Central. Our warehouse owner was doing a disappearing act with our lease money. Panic set in as locked doors and an impending pickup deadline had us sweating more than a jalapeño in July.

Thank the tequila gods for nice management companies! They swooped in like angels, unlocked the gates, and saved our precious cargo just in the nick of time. Crisis averted, but not without a mountain of paperwork, moving chaos, and nail-biting anxiety as we waited for a new liquor license in order to secure another warehouse.

But all's well that ends well, and we began a love affair with our new warehouse. It's like finding the perfect dance partner. We've got a fantastic relationship with this new place. It's proof that sometimes, just sometimes, the tequila stars align in our favor. Cheers to that!

"Above the Stars" captures the turmoil of shipping and storage with an ice cube that is stamped with an "S" and cucumber skin that mimics the shrink-wrapping hassles. But it finishes sweet and light with cucumber, pear, and Lillet Rose, just as our search for a new warehouse did.

# A Dance of Inspiration

## Ingredients

1 oz. Añejo tequila

1 oz. Lillet Blanc

1 ½ oz. fresh orange juice

¼ oz. Ancho Reyes liquor

1 tsp. local honey

Add all ingredients into a Boston Shaker tin with ice and shake vigorously. Strain into a Riedel Coupe glass. Garnish with an edible blue tuile wafer

## SHARING TEQUILA …
## IS SHARING LIFE

The love we received from the consumers ignited a spark within us, a thrill that made every tasting and event feel like a celebration. Each sale wasn't just a transaction; it was a lifeline that allowed us to keep our dreams alive. There were times it didn't even feel like work because our passion flowed freely through every interaction.

As entrepreneurs, we wore many hats, but the greatest joy came from being with our community. The laughter, the shared stories—it was a dance of inspiration that lit up our hearts. Jon at one store, me at another, but always with the same purpose. At the end of each day, we would sink into our couch, glasses raised, toasting to the gratitude that filled our souls as we savored Señor Rio together.

Behind each bottle lies a hidden truth: "Sharing Tequila... Is Sharing Life." We chose this message with intention, a gentle reminder not to take a single moment for granted. It's tucked away behind the labels, waiting for you to discover it, just as life's deeper meanings often are.

We invite you to open your bottle, to share Señor Rio with those you love—family, friends, anyone who makes your heart feel full. In those moments, as you sip and savor, may you find the courage to share your own stories, to weave together memories that transcend time. Tomorrow is never guaranteed, but each toast brings us closer, connecting generations just as it did with my father and us. So, let's celebrate life together, one sip at a time.

A Dance of Inspiration captures the true essence and meaning behind the bottle. The rich warmness of the patiently aged Añejo and sweet natural honey compliments the dance on the palate with a bit of spice and vibrant orange adding depth just like each experience of life's rhythm.

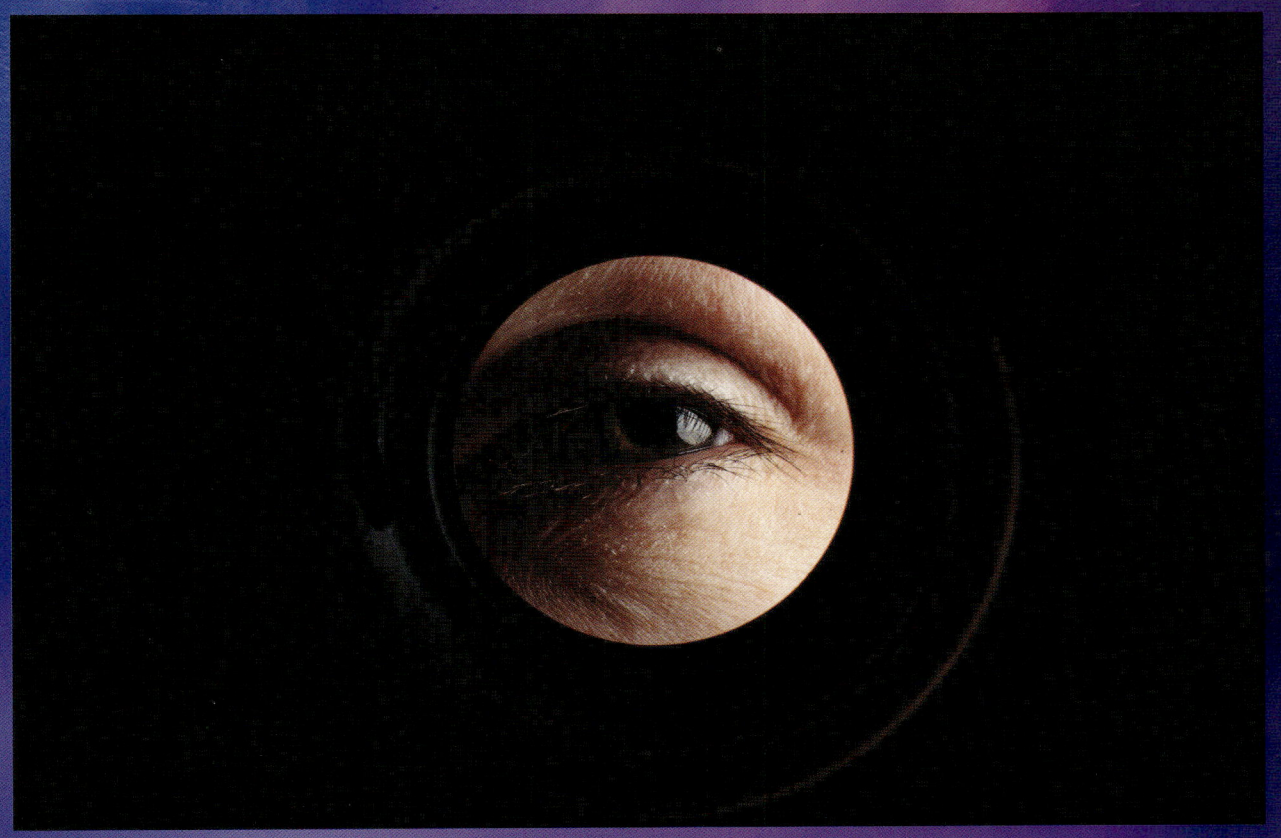

# Paper Planes

# Ingrediants

2 oz. Blanco tequila

2 oz. pistachio liquor

1 oz. fresh lime juice

2 dashes of Fee Brothers orange bitters

Dress the rocks glass with agave syrup and dust with crushed pistachios. Add all ingredients into a Boston Shaker tin with ice and shake vigorously. Strain into a cocktail rocks glass with a large ice cube. Top with lime air (2 oz. fresh lime juice, 1 ½ tsp. sucrose, 1 ½ tsp. salt, blended with immersion blender—a molecular gastronomy technique). Garnish with a paper plane on the rim.

# A CELEBRITY, PLEASE

We decided to take the plunge into the wild world of celebrity endorsements and chase the elusive star-studded nod for Señor Rio. Armed with an elegant bottle and a smooth taste that could charm even the pickiest palates, we embarked on a journey through the maze of fame.

First stop: the realm of unreachable celebs. We dove into Google, but all we found were PR agencies looking for cash, not endorsements. It was like trying to catch a unicorn with a fishing net!

Our next step was to seek out local talent. A marketing company we contacted in Arizona promised the moon and stars, yet our pockets weren't deep enough for their stellar services. We needed an investor first, they said. So, we waited, like tequila aging in oak barrels.

Then, a glimmer of hope came through a web of connections, and we were promised a meeting with an A-list celeb we were to meet at the Daytona Beach Rolex race. We packed our bags, booked flights, and even found a condo thanks to some leftover timeshare magic.

But hold the lime! Our marketing buddy (who stayed with us in the condo we reserved) turned into a peanut-eating fiend at night, leaving shells everywhere like a messy squirrel. Then came the big reveal: our celeb rendezvous turned out to be a sponsorship pitch for race cars with a price tag of $70,000 per race. We were pouring tequila, not printing money!

Still, we were there already, so we returned to the races, literally and figuratively. Unfortunately, our marketing mate's greed for self-promotion left a bitter taste in our mouths as he mingled our meeting with his own interests.

Fast forward to New York where we waltzed into the world of TV production. Product placement? Sure! Equity in exchange? Maybe. But our brand got sidelined for another tequila as the contract dance turned into a pirouette of broken promises.

Back in California at a charity event, we donated plenty of cases and were invited to their VIP section. We found ourselves rubbing elbows with reality TV royalty and shaking hands with rockstars incognito. However, we left with no connections.

Charity events and failed sponsorships led us to set our sights on Shark Tank.

After several submissions, we got the hint: tequila wasn't their cup of tea. But rejection didn't dampen our spirits.

Through ups and downs, rejections, and near-misses, one thing remained constant: our passion for Señor Rio and the belief that someday, somehow, we'd find our place in the spotlight, one sip at a time.

"Paper Planes without Peanuts" is a nod to our self-indulgent marketing buddy, but with a healthier and more positive twist through pistachios. And the molecular gastronomy addition elevates the cocktail further.

# MR. MIAMI

## INGREDIENTS

1 oz. Blanco tequila

1 oz. simple syrup

2 slices of cucumber

1 oz. Pataka cucumber liqueur

1 oz. fresh lime juice

Fever Tree Lime Mexican soda

Fresh mint sprigs

Dress a collins glass with four fresh mint sprigs and ice cubes. Add all ingredients into a Boston Shaker tin with ice and shake vigorously. Strain into the glass. Top the cocktail with Fever Tree lime Mexican soda. Garnish with a cucumber peel and fresh mint.

# A CONSULTANT

Ah, the wild and wacky world of industry veterans and their pie-in-the-sky promises! Someone we knew in the industry referred us to a seasoned pro-turned consultant from the big leagues who had decided to dive into the small brand scene, and he came armed with assurances of CEO connections and industry insights that could make our brand soar to new heights.

We rolled out the red carpet, or in this case, the Arizona desert sands, for this promising ally. Airline tickets? Check. Hotel reservations? Check. We were ready to rock and roll with this potential game-changer.

Despite his polished pitches and confident vibes, reality hit hard. The contacts he claimed to have ghosted him, and he didn't deliver on anything he proposed to us. The problem was that when he left to start his consulting firm, he thought his list of business associates would be resourceful contacts to help grow brands. Instead, they cut off his access, and he could not deliver even a meeting with them.

Mr. Miami also had said he was friends with Emilio and Gloria Estefan. Being a big fan of the artist and her husband, I sent a bottle and a heartfelt note to Gloria Estefan, the queen of inspirational tunes and conga line memories.

So, here's to laughing at the curveballs, finding inspiration wherever you can, and keeping the tequila flowing even when the industry's antics throw you for a loop. It's a reminder that even in the glamorous world of spirits and showbiz, relation-ships can be quite fickle. Who knows? Maybe Gloria got my message.

"Mr. Miami" takes the iconic mojito that represents Miami and gives it our unique tequila twist, once again finding the bright side of our challenging road.

## *Ingredients*

1 oz. Blanco tequila

1 oz. peach puree

2 oz. Prosecco

1/2 oz. agave nectar

Fresh peach wedges

Add all ingredients except Prosecco into a Boston Shaker tin with ice and shake vigorously. Strain into a fancy crystal glass. Top with Prosecco and garnish with four slices of peach wedges.

# 2-D

The song titled "Class in a Glass" not only became a catchy anthem but also forged a unique connection with an artist chasing his dreams. The song's narrative, intertwined with the allure of Señor Rio tequila, added a vibrant and personal touch to our brand. The lyrics told a story of how an average guy at a bar gets a Designer Diva's attention with his bottle of Señor Rio. The pairing of 2-D, the artist from south Phoenix who rhymes with fast-talking rap, and the beat of one of my favorite jazz songs—"Rainforest" by Paul Hardcastle—was the perfect mix.

Fortunately, the internet assisted in locating and reaching out to the infamous Mr. Hardcastle, and he graciously agreed to our using his music for promotional use only. We were beyond grateful and thrilled, offering to send him a few of our bottles in exchange for his kindness.

Being that he resides in the UK, he asked if we would send them to a friend of his in California, as it would be complicated to ship alcohol to him overseas. Amazing what can be accomplished with tequila and sharing your love of an artist's music. "You can't get kissed unless you ask." "Class in a Glass" is available on the senorrio.com website in the music section tab.

"Class in a Glass" addresses the craving for something refreshing and crisp that comes from wanting more, such as a luxury lifestyle. A unique way of doing that is incorporating Prosecco and peaches with the fruitful Blanco tequila. We added our ingredients into a vintage classic wine glass for a touch of class.

## Class in a Glass

Music by Paul Hardcastle

Lyrics by 2-D

# Mexican Mai Tai

## Ingredientes

1 oz. Blanco tequila

1 oz. Pierre Ferrand Dry Curacao orange liqueur

1 oz. Giffard grenadine

½ oz. Giffard orgeat

Add all ingredients into a Boston Shaker tin with ice and shake vigorously. Strain into a Riedel double cocktail rocks glass with regular ice cubes. Float a dash of extra grenadine and garnish with an edible flower.

# ESCAPE WITH SEÑOR RIO

When Jon and I could afford to eat out, we always made a beeline for the restaurants that served Señor Rio. However, dining out was a luxury because money was usually tighter than Jon's old skinny jeans. On one of our cherished date nights, we found ourselves at a cozy spot where the bartender had a knack for crafting divine Señor Rio cocktails. This guy was all about small-batch tequila, and he made a special cocktail for me that was so good, it deserved its own fan club.

As we sipped our drinks and savored our dinner, the live music set the perfect ambiance. There were two guitarists whose performance was so incredible they should've come with their own applause track. On our way out, I couldn't resist stopping to tell them how much we loved their music. I handed them my card and said, "We make tequila, you make beautiful music. Let's make magic together."

Believe it or not, they called! We ended up collaborating on a CD titled *Escape with Señor Rio* that became a promotional giveaway featuring Spanish guitar with a Flamenco flair. The best part is that what started as a business relationship blossomed into a genuine friendship. Sometimes, the universe sends you wonderful people just when you need them most. These musicians even

played at the cocktail hour for my daughter's wedding day, adding a personal touch to the celebration.

To this day, we still give away that CD, and recently we thought about selling it in a local shop. We reached out to Charles, one of the guitarists, for his blessing. He responded eagerly, "Sure, sell them! Just remember, when you make a million, send me to Hawaii." Now that's what I call a sweet deal!

The "Mexican Mai Tai" is an homage to the talented guitarist who partnered with us and had the simple request that he get a trip to Hawaii. This was my way of sweeping him away to the tropics, and I hope it will do the same for you.

# JON'S PICASO

1 oz. Reposado tequila

1 oz. Pierre Ferrand Dry Curacao orange liqueur

1 oz. Chareau aloe liqueur

1 oz. fresh lemon juice

2 dashes of Fee Brothers peach bitters

Add all ingredients into a Boston Shaker tin with ice and shake vigorously. Strain into a champagne flute. Garnish with blue tuile wafer.

# A TOAST TO ANDY

While hosting a tequila tasting in Arizona at a local bar and having a blast chatting with everyone, we met a guy named Andy who said he was an artist. We joked, "How about painting our bottles sometime?" He grinned, tipped his top hat, and said, "Sure, for tequila!" He didn't even want the bottles for himself—they were

ful and stunning, and we made posters to use in future tastings. They were a hit at bars but a bit too spicy for some venues.

Our friendship with Andy blossomed, and he continued to lend his talents to our promotional efforts. On one occasion, he painted a chair for a charity auction at a Mexican restaurant, telling our story with colorful folk art. The chair, paired with our tequila, sold for a few hundred ward, we drove two hours to Tucson for the Rotary event where they surprised us with a birthday cake. We were thrilled but exhausted.

To top it off, Jon's brother Robert gifted us a trip to Las Vegas where we stayed at the Bellagio in a gorgeous suite. We enjoyed a fantastic dinner and show thanks to Robert's generosity. It was a birthday to remember!

That year, my daughters and I surprised Jon with an original painting by Andy of our Señor Rio bottle and a cigar. It's our very own Picasso and hangs proudly in Jon's office. RIP Andy. You remain in my heart.

"Jon's Picasso" is an elevated cocktail of artistic proportions to be enjoyed in a champagne flute. This toast to Andy is a celebration of good friends and creative endeavors.

The Frenchman

## Ingredients

1 oz. Añejo tequila

1 oz. Grand Marnier

1 oz. Chambord

1 oz. fresh blood orange juice

1 oz. fresh lime juice

1 tsp. agave syrup

Add all ingredients into a Boston Shaker tin with ice and shake vigorously. Strain into a champagne flute. Garnish with red tuile wafer.

# SHANGHAI DELIGHT

Our bottle guy, Stanley, who seemed so promising, turned out to be a disaster. Bottles and stoppers were arriving broken in Mexico because his packing was atrocious. The damage kept increasing, and half the Extra Añejo bottles in our latest order were shattered. They were not protected with bubble wrap—just tossed into cardboard boxes.

We knew we had to cut ties. We needed a reliable supplier, so Jon and I started researching companies in China. We emailed multiple firms, asking about minimum orders, production time, mold costs, references, etc. We found our top three and booked flights to Shanghai.

A couple who were friends of ours decided to join us on our "business" trip. After a 12-hour flight from LA, we arrived in Shanghai only to find our ride did not show. Great start! We found our own way to the hotel, checked in, and later explored the area, enjoying a seafood feast.

The next morning, we had our first meeting with a bottle company. We were greeted by the owner, a sophisticated Frenchman who had started his own bottle company after frustrations in the liquor industry. His fiancée, who was much younger and spoke perfect English, joined us later. The meeting went well, and the bottle quality was impressive.

That evening, they took us to Mr. and Mrs. Bund, an upscale French restaurant. The food was divine, the service exceptional, and the atmosphere oozed luxury. We felt spoiled! After dinner, we enjoyed champagne on the rooftop with sparklers—quite the experience!

Later, we hit a Cuban Havana nightclub with their account manager and his wife who had relocated from Spain to Shanghai. The energy was electrifying, and Jon got to smoke cigars, which made him incredibly happy.

The next day, we sealed the deal with the Frenchman. His company would supply our bottles and stoppers, solving our quality issues. We canceled our other appointments and enjoyed the rest of the trip with our friends, shopping and dining. To this day, we're happy with our decision, and no more broken bottles!

"The Frenchman" uses inspired ingredients from France like the Grand Marnier and Chambord paired with the award-wining Añejo, all presented in a champagne flute for a Cheers! or Santé! to the Famous Frenchman.

# NO CIGAR

2 oz. Reposado tequila

1 oz. Pama liqueur

2 oz. POM pomegranate juice

1 oz. fresh lime juice

1 tsp. agave syrup

Add all ingredients into a Boston Shaker tin with ice and shake vigorously. Strain into a Riedel coupe glass. Top with a smoke bubble from a smoke gun. (The Flavor Blaster smoke gun, accompanied with their smoke and bubble products is recommended.)

# THE AÑEJO AND DIAMANTE

Jonathan was a cigar enthusiast for three decades, following in his dad's smoky footsteps, and had the brilliant idea to infuse cigars with our tequila for promotional giveaways. We printed Señor Rio cigar bands, bought a few bundles, and infused them by storing them with a glass of Blanco tequila. The aroma was heavenly as we banded each cigar and stored them in our humidor for tasting events. They were a hit, boosting our bottle sales.

Jon always dreamed of creating his own cigar blend and, in 2014, we ventured to Nicaragua to make it happen. We met A.J. Fernandez and his team in Estelí, staying in guest quarters with housekeepers and cooks. They gave us a tour, taught us the art of rolling cigars (we were terrible at it), and introduced us to their superstar roller who could roll 300 cigars a day.

Jon crafted the Señor Rio Añejo cigar to perfection while I created the Señor Rio Diamante—a smaller, creamy cigar dedicated to my daughters who both got married in 2014. We secured a purchase order from Total Wine and were thrilled to add cigars to our product line. Our trip was educational and fun. We built great relationships and had a custom humidor made to store the cigars in Arizona.

Despite our efforts, selling the cigars was tough. Many cigar shops were uninterested, but a few did place orders. We needed reviews to break into the cliquish cigar industry; and, to our delight, we received positive feedback. Señor Rio cigars, handmade in Nicaragua, were praised for their

exquisite quality. The Añejo was perfect with tequila, and the Diamante, intended for women, actually became a unisex favorite.

Despite their success, we decided not to continue producing cigars, focusing instead on what works best—Señor Rio tequila. If you find one of our cigars, savor it; they were made with love and are now a rare, aged delicacy. Ultimately, sticking with our bread and butter was the best move.

"No Cigar" features the sweet notes and heavy flavors that can hold up to the potent aroma of smoke. Elevating the cocktail with texture and the extra smoke element pays homage to Jon.

# A Toast to Jalisco

# Ingredients

2 oz. Reposado tequila

1 oz. Flying Leap habanero brandy liqueur

1 oz. fresh lime juice

1 oz. agave syrup

A fresh cilantro sprig

Dress a gold-rimmed margarita glass with fresh lime juice and dust with Tajin Clasico mild lime seasoning. Add all ingredients into a Boston Shaker tin with ice and shake vigorously. Strain into the glass. Garnish with two dehydrated limes.

# Queen of the South

One morning, while scrolling through Facebook, I spotted a post with a woman holding our tequila bottle. Comments flooded in from friends and aquaintances: "Hey, is that your bottle?" I showed Jonathan, and we both agreed—it was definitely ours. Turns out, the show "Queen of the South" on the USA Network used our Señor Rio bottle in a few scenes. To our surprise, they had renamed it and claimed it was a $2,000 bottle. We couldn't help but laugh and say, "Cool!"

Naturally, we had to binge-watch the show. It's addictive, heart-pounding, and packed with cartel madness. Since the first episode aired in June 2016, we only had to catch up to season two. If you haven't tuned in yet, check it out on Netflix—it's a wild ride from start to finish.

We started following the show on social media and even emailed them, thanking them for featuring our bottle and offering more. We got no response; but, hey, we loved the show and continued to watch it. It would have been nice if they'd left our label on, though!

The cast truly brought their characters to life. Bravo to Alice Braga, Veronica Falcon, Peter Gadiot, Joaquim de Almeida, Hemky Madera, Justina Machado, Gerardo Taracena, Jon-Michael Ecker, and Molly Burnett. Their performances were incredible, and we were true fans.

A huge thank you to the executive producers for featuring our bottle in the July 20, 2017, Season 2, Episode 7, titled "El Precio de la Fe." Cheers to a great show!

"A Toast to Jalisco" is a nod to the show "Queen of the South" that is set in the barrio of Jalisco, Mexico. This classic margarita is punched up with modern glassware. Salud!

# Risky Business

## Ingredients

1 ½ oz. Blanco tequila

1 oz. Cointreau

1 oz. fresh lime juice

1 oz. fresh orange juice

1 ½ oz. Real coconut syrup

Add all ingredients into a Boston Shaker tin with ice and shake vigorously. Strain into a cocktail rocks glass. Garnish with fresh edible flowers.

# STAYING ALIVE

Before becoming a Spirits Direct item at Total Wine & More, we struggled to keep our business and personal finances afloat. For the first five years, we didn't earn an income. We relied on savings, family, and credit cards to get by. Mr. Visa and Mr. Mastercard came to the rescue when ends didn't meet, and we even sold valuables when gold prices were high. I visited those infamous "We Buy Gold" shops with my treasured jewelry I purchased during my real estate days.

Jonathan did the same, parting with rings he never wore, and even his eighty-year-old mother gave us jewelry to sell. We vowed to do whatever it took to keep our business alive. Eventually, our credit cards were maxed out, and we could only make minimum payments with interest rates as high as 29%.

However, even as we struggled, reading about other startup liquor companies inspired us. Tito's Vodka founder, Tito Beveridge, maxed out his credit cards to $70,000 before his vodka took off. Jim Koch of Samuel Adams brewed his first beer in his kitchen, and now sells millions of barrels annually. John Paul DeJoria, co-founder of Patron Tequila, started with a small batch and now dominates the premium tequila market. Jon and I believed in each other and our dream, despite the bittersweet, complicated, and stressful journey. Starting a business is risky, but it's working out. Are we a success story? We think so. We're still here, trucking along, one bottle at a time.

"Risky Business" plays with textures and highlights coconut in this cocktail as a way of acknowledging the rocky road of entrepreneurship and the little touch of "coconuts" it takes to take on a venture like this.

Le Bristol

## Ingredients

1 oz. Blanco tequila

1 oz. fresh lemon juice

champagne

Add all ingredients except champagne into a Boston Shaker tin with ice and shake vigorously. Strain into a champagne flute. Top with champagne. Garnish with a lemon peel shaped as a crown, using a gold cocktail pick to keep it together.

# Paris Will Always Be There

Jon and I had been dating for a few years and were truly soulmates. Marriage was important to us, but we felt no pressure, believing we'd know the right time to take that step. We already felt committed in our hearts and had a strong partnership. Did we need a piece of paper to validate our relationship?

I had been married for seventeen years, so we took it slow. One day in 2014, Jon, a lifelong bachelor, decided to surprise me with a well-executed proposal. He caught me off guard after returning from a trip to New York. He mentioned a package was coming and asked me to put it in his office when it arrived, which I did without question. Little did I know he was shopping in the NY diamond district for my ring and the package that arrived would mark our next step toward marriage.

Later, he suggested we plan a Christmas party and made a reservation at Dominick's Steakhouse in Scottsdale, Arizona. He insisted I wear a new sparkly dress, which I reluctantly agreed to. That night, we had a beautiful dinner, and when I returned from the ladies' room, there was champagne and dessert on the table. Jon then pulled out a ring box and proposed. I was stunned and, of course, said yes. The ring was beautiful, and we toasted to our future.

We had a long engagement as my daughters were busy with their own growing families. But we decided on a destination wedding in Paris in June 2017. My daughters encouraged us to follow our dream, and Jon's brother generously offered to cover our wedding expenses in Paris. We chose Le Bristol for our fairy-tale celebration.

Knowing my daughters and grandchildren would not be able

to make the trip to Paris, we decided to have an intimate wedding ceremony in Arizona of 16 guests in April before the Paris trip.

However, Jon began experiencing severe stomach pain, and after several tests, he was diagnosed with stage-four pancreatic cancer. This news came eleven days before our Arizona ceremony was planned. We were devastated, and it was as if our lives came to a stop. There are no words to describe what we felt. However, we decided to proceed with our Arizona wedding. Jon began treatment right after at the Virginia G. Piper Cancer Center, which became our second home. We ended up postponing our Paris trip. Despite the challenges, we remained hopeful and continued to support each other through every step.

"Le Bristol" is our version of the French 75 classic cocktail that originated in the New York Bar in Paris, bringing a little bit of Jon into the mix with our tequila.

# BITTERSWEET

## Ingredients

1 oz. Añejo tequila

1 oz. Grand Marnier

2 oz. fresh lemon juice

1 oz. Real strawberry

1 oz. POM pomegranate juice

2 dashes of Fee Brothers orange bitters

Add all ingredients into a Boston Shaker tin with ice and shake vigorously. Strain into a Zwiesel wine glass. Garnish with a red and tan tuile wafer held together by a gold pin.

# COCO AND CHANEL

Jon's cancer treatment led to many side effects and hospital stays, which was difficult on our Shih Tzu poodles, Coco and Chanel, since we were often away. During one hospital stay, a nurse asked if we had children or pets. We told her about our grandchildren and the dogs. She shared that her boys, aged six and eight, were begging for dogs, but she wanted small breeds. When she mentioned loving Shih Tzus, I showed her pictures of Coco and Chanel.

That night, I suggested to Jon that maybe this nurse was meant to find us. Our dogs needed more attention than we could give, and her family seemed perfect for them. With a heavy heart, I proposed the idea of her adopting Coco and Chanel. I tossed and turned that night, unsure if it was the right decision.

The next morning, I asked the nurse if she'd be interested in our dogs. She was thrilled but wanted to check with her husband. When she returned with a positive response, we arranged for her to visit. Coco and Chanel took to her immediately, and I gathered their belongings, holding back tears as I hugged her.

What began as a trial run turned permanent. It felt like giving up children for adoption, but I knew it was best for our dogs. A few weeks later, she returned with

her boys to pick up a doggie door, sharing that Coco and Chanel were doing great. While it's bittersweet, I believe people come into our lives for a reason, and this was meant to be.

"Bittersweet" offers comforting flavors reminiscent of the warm and thoughtful place we were in as we said a painful goodbye to our beloved dogs, knowing it was best for everyone.

Lucky 13

## Ingredients

2 oz. Blanco tequila

1 oz. Giffard sour apple liqueur

2 oz. fresh lemon juice

1 oz. simple syrup

1 oz. Real apple syrup

2 slices of jalapeño

Add all ingredients into a Boston Shaker tin with ice and shake vigorously. Strain into a Fortes Jupiter highball glass with regular ice cubes. Garnish with a lime peel rolled into a flower, held together by a gold cocktail pick in the center.

# His Lucky Number

The treatment Jon received for his cancer was called the Grand Slam. It was an aggressive, five-drug regimen combining chemotherapy, immunotherapy, and a special form of vitamin D. The days at the cancer center were long, and Jon was a trooper. I called him my brave warrior, taking on this terrorist called cancer. These treatments were like dropping explosive bombs in your body, hoping to eliminate the enemy.

As he signed the dotted lines consenting to this clinical trial, knowing there is no cure, I asked how many patients were in the trial. The response was, "We are only taking twenty-four patients." I asked what number Jon was. He was number 13. We looked at each other in amazement because 13 was his lucky number—he even had it tattooed on his arm.

*Wow, that's a good sign from the universe*, I thought. Jon always kept a sense of humor, even in the darkest days of his battle. I remember when the doctor asked if he had any questions, and

Jon looked him straight in the face and said, "Yeah, do you know why Italians don't like Jehovah's Witnesses?" The doctor scratched his head and answered, "No, I don't." Not realizing he was being set up, Jon grinned and said, "It's because they don't like any witnesses." Even during this very difficult time, Jon always put a smile on someone's face.

"Lucky 13" features the quintessential lucky color: green. But it is also a tall drink, a little sour like the news of Jon's cancer. Luck can turn from sweet to sour, and this cocktail has elements of both.

# Eternal Spirits

## Ingredients

1 oz. Reposado tequila

2 oz. fresh grapefruit juice

1 oz. lychee juice

2 spoonfuls of lychee sherbet

Add all ingredients into a Boston Shaker tin with ice and shake vigorously. Strain into a Riedel Nick and Nora glass. Garnish with a green roots tuile wafer held together by a gold pin.

# Until We Meet Again

Jon and I had such a beautiful journey together, though it included a true roller coaster of emotions. Our bond grew stronger than ever through the cancer diagnosis, and our family was incredibly supportive as we leaned on each other. We took things one day at a time, reflecting on our humble beginnings from business to friendship to love. We struggled financially but never faced any major health issues. We had no idea of what was to come

In November 2017, Jon was at the end of his sixth cycle of cancer treatments. Since his diagnosis in April, we had been coming to the Cancer Center three days a week for 10-hour days. He was my warrior, and I am still so very proud of him. To pass the time, Jon enjoyed watching the Food Network, whether it was Andrew Zimmern or Guy Fieri. The Food Network channel became our refuge, providing a comforting escape from the infusions.

I remember asking Jon if there was anything monumental, he would like to do after his treatments were over. He said he wanted to smoke a cigar with Arnold Schwarzenegger and Sylvester Stallone. I would have given anything to make that dream a reality. If only there were a Make-A-Wish Foundation for adults. Cancer is a terrible disease, but one thing I've learned is that it does not define you. It makes you stronger.

I want to thank the Cancer Center for their compassion, support, and treatments. My beloved Jonathan left this earth in February 2018. We had thirteen extraordinary years together, and his spirit lives on every day in my heart. When someone asks, "Where is your husband?" I smile and say, "He's in Heaven; and aren't we all just trying to get there one day?"

"Eternal Spirits" is a dream cocktail that can be a part of a night in on the couch, watching a movie. It uses ingredients you can keep in the freezer or refrigerator. It showcases how elevating the cocktails at home can be fun too. This cocktail is made to be enjoyed with someone special to savor the precious time we have together.

# TEQUILA SMILES

## INGREDIENTS

2 oz. Reposado tequila

1 oz. St. Germain elderflower liqueur

2 oz. fresh lemon juice

1 oz. Real raspberry syrup

Add all ingredients into a Boston Shaker tin with ice and shake vigorously. Strain into a champagne glass. Garnish with a large raspberry gummy speared with a gold cocktail pick in the center.

# WATCHING OVER ME

After Jonathan's passing, I was consumed by deep grief. People would often ask, "Are you going to sell the Tequila company? What are you going to do now?" My immediate response was, "No, this is something we built together. I will continue his legacy."

Grief counseling through the church and the unwavering support of my family comforted me immensely; however, being in the stores truly helped me cope with my loss because I genuinely love what I do.

Fortunately, I had a few incredible brand ambassadors who went above and beyond to help me host tastings and traveled with me to different markets. Irma and Rosa, I can't thank you enough for your support and genuine friendship.

I am blessed to have a close family and dear friends who I consider family. They inspire me to believe in myself and that anything is possible. I travel 2-3 times a month, sampling and sharing the Señor Rio story one bottle at a time. The stores are always welcoming, and I love spreading tequila smiles. I feel Jon's presence at times and know he is watching over me.

I've experienced both successes and losses on this journey, and I am grateful every day. I am confident that Señor Rio is here to stay. It is truly because of you that we are still here, and I thank you from the bottom of my heart for embracing a small, minority woman-owned business.

"Tequila Smiles" has elderflower and raspberries, ingredients that represent joy and love. Topping it with a raspberry gummy gives it an extra dose of fun and appreciation for life, just as Jon did in my life. We are all still smiling with you, Jon. Salud!!!

BRING AWARENESS

# Ingredients

2 oz. Blanco tequila
1 oz. Grand Marnier liqueur
2 oz. fresh lemon juice
1 oz. prickly pear syrup
2 dashes Fee Brothers orange bitters

Add all ingredients into a Boston Shaker tin with ice and shake vigorously. Strain into a gold-rimmed margarita glass with a large ice cube or regular ice. Garnish with a blue tuile wafer on the side of the rim.

# WE CARE CRUSADE

In 2020, I could not visit the stores during Covid—in-person tastings were not an option—and I was fearful of how this would impact sales. I was homebound like a lot of people, working remotely, running the company from the computer. I focused on developing our digital footprint by revising the website and figuring out social media.

I cherish the time with my family and am extremely proud of my two amazing daughters, Crystal and Tiffany, and my sons-in-law Kevin and Paul who have blessed me with seven beautiful grandchildren from ten years old to one year old. My identical twin granddaughters, Katalina and Klaudia, are my nine-year-old heroes who both have special needs. They were diagnosed with Angelman syndrome, cerebral palsy, and autism. They can light up a room immediately with their smiles despite being nonverbal.

In honor of my granddaughters, I founded a non-profit foundation, We Care Crusade, dedicated to helping families who have children with special needs. It's a small foundation and is funded by Señor Rio tequila. For each bottle sold, one dollar goes into We Care Crusade. We want to make a difference one child at a time, one family at a time, one bottle at a time to lighten their life with some form of relief—medically, physically, and emotionally.

I have immense admiration for the families facing these challenges every day, knowing they were given a gift from above in raising God's special children. It is the little things that make the biggest impact. If you or another family needs assistance. Please reach out to us at Wecarecrusade.org. We are also donating a portion from the sale of each copy of *One Bottle at a Time* to We Care Crusade.

"Bring Awareness" is a simple cocktail that brings Arizona to the forefront. We are known for our prickly pear, and it is a fantastic addition to the classic margarita to bring awareness to our important cause. Simple yet elegant. Salud!

# THE MAXWELL

## INGREDIENTS

1 oz. Reposado tequila

1 oz. Gran Ponche Mexicano pomegranate liqueur

1 oz. Grand Marnier liqueur

2 oz. fresh orange juice

1 oz. Giffard Vanilla de Madagascar liqueur

Add all ingredients into a Boston Shaker tin with ice and shake vigorously. Strain into a vintage crystal goblet with a large ice cube. Garnish with a dehydrated orange slice hung from a small gold clothespin on the side of the glass.

Guy and gifted him a bottle of Señor Rio. His genuine empathy moved me deeply, and we took a photo together, each holding a bottle—one from his brand, one from mine.

Determined to make the most of the day, I stayed to host a tequila tasting at the wine bar. As I waited for customers, I noticed they were mostly there for Guy—snapping photos and leaving with his signed bottles. Just when I thought it would be a quiet day, a strikingly handsome gentleman caught my eye. He approached, intrigued by my tequila. We struck up a conversation and he introduced himself as Jack Maxwell, mentioning that he was shopping for a gift for his doctor.

In 2023, my business was flourishing, and I found myself back in stores, sharing my passion for tequila. During a bottle signing at Total Wine in Arizona, fate stepped in when I met Guy Fieri. My late husband, Jon, had adored Guy's shows, finding solace in them during his cancer treatments. With a heart full of gratitude, I shared this with

As we chatted, I shared my story—how I was honoring Jon's memory on this day, expressing how much he had loved Guy's shows. Jack listened with compassion, revealing his own battle with cancer and how he was one of the fortunate ones who had come through it. Our connection deepened with each word, and I felt a comforting bond forming between us.

We exchanged contact information and soon met for brunch. Jack's infectious positivity made it feel like we had known each other forever. During our meal, I confided in him about my search for a business partner. Jack listened intently and offered to introduce me to someone he knew: Joe Mantegna. I had no idea at the time that Jack was the host of a show called "Booze Traveler," exploring the world of spirits and stories.

Looking back, I can't help but feel that Jon led Jack to me, opening the door to Joe. I'm incredibly grateful for Jack's kindness and am honored to call him a friend.

From this serendipitous connection, "The Maxwell" cocktail was born—bold and charismatic, just like Jack. It brings together vibrant flavors that complement each other, much like our friendship. Next time you're hosting, serve this drink to spark lively conversations—it's perfect for casual gatherings and will have everyone coming back for more.

DAZAZA

# Ingredients

2 oz. Señor Rio liqueur tequila
1 oz. Luxardo espresso liqueur
1 oz. Mozart White Classico
2 scoops Dos Leches ice cream

---

Add all ingredients into a Boston Shaker tin, shake vigorously. Add some ice and shake twice. Strain into Riedel Coupe glass. Top with chocolate shaved with a microplane.

## LADIES AND GENTLEMEN, MR. JOE MANTEGNA

As fate would have it, I met Mr. Joe Mantegna. Nervous yet confident, I shared my story about starting the company with Jonathan, paying tribute to my dad, and bringing a three-generation-old recipe to market. It was no easy feat, but what a journey it's been.

After Jon's passing, I remained dedicated to our dream. Joe listened intently, asked a few questions, and when I spoke about We Care Crusade and my desire to help families in need, he was deeply moved.

We connected over our Chicago roots and his experience raising a daughter with special needs. He tasted the tequila, appreciating its all-natural quality. Then, he said the words that changed everything: "I like your tequila. I believe in you and what you stand for. It's a tequila with a cause. I'm in . . . just one thing." My heart raced, fearing a daunting request, but he simply said, "You just have to meet my wife." Thankfully, she liked me.

Having Joe as a business partner and co-owner has been instrumental in growing the brand. His bottle signings draw crowds with lines out the door, not just because he's a celebrity but because he is a genuinely good person. His compassion for each person he meets makes me proud to know him. Joe's passion for helping active service members, veterans, first responders, and individuals with special needs is inspiring. Despite his fame from over 300 films and nearly eighteen years on *Criminal Minds*, his dedication to our small tequila company is heartwarming.

I am fortunate to know Joe, his family, and his friend/producing manager Dan Ramm. Thank you, Joe, for all that you do.

Da Za Za closes our tour of handcrafted tequila cocktails on a sweet note. Señor Rio is taken to a new level with the inclusion of cordials. The Blanco with arabica coffee beans is a great addition to an espresso style martini. Incorporating dos leches ice cream, white chocolate liqueur, espresso liqueur, and your favorite dark chocolate to top it off create a perfect dessert or pick-me-up, whether out on the town or enjoying a night in.

# CLOSING

Just when I thought everything was falling into place, a seismic jolt shook my world. On July 25, 2024, I received a letter from the attorney's office representing the warehouse where I stored thousands of tequila cases. I had to read the letter three times before the reality sunk in, and with each pass, tears blurred the words. The warehouse had been devastated by a storm, the roof had collapsed, and every single case of tequila—about 5,000 cases, valued at close to $1 million—was destroyed.

The letter was a harsh blow, but it didn't stop there. It went on to explain that because the warehouse was a leased space, their insurance wouldn't cover the loss. I immediately reached out to my insurance carrier only to discover that the coverage was woefully inadequate. For years, I had simply paid the premiums without ever being advised to adjust my coverage as my business grew. I had been so engrossed in expanding the company, building our brand, and managing every detail that I overlooked this critical aspect.

My late husband Jonathan, who always handled these matters, had set up our insurance coverage over a decade ago, reflecting our needs at that time. As our business expanded, so did our inventory, but the insurance remained at the same level. Now, faced with the loss of every bottle of tequila we had—each one a testament to years of hard work and dedication—it felt like a death.

Yet, amidst the devastation, a more profound sorrow struck. A young employee, a father with a newborn son, lost his life in the collapse. My heart aches for his family, particularly for his son who will grow up without him. Such tragedies transform everything into a surreal nightmare.

Despite the heartbreak and the seemingly insurmountable challenges, I was determined to rebuild. Señor Rio isn't just a brand; it is a symbol of love, family, and legacy. Our story is far from over. Señor Rio will endure and thrive, honoring the past and embracing the future with renewed vigor.

# HOW SEÑOR RIO TEQUILA IS MADE

Señor Rio tequila is made with love and tradition, beginning with the farming of the blue weber agave plant. The agaves are harvested in the lowlands of Jalisco in the town of Tequila, Mexico. They mature in a red volcanic clay soil over 8 to 12 years. Cultivation requires the temperature to remain stable at 68 degrees and they are grown some 5,000 feet above sea level.

All of our agaves are from one single estate. Keeping them in the earth that long gives them the proper sugar content, which yields a smoother taste. We do not add anything artificial. Even the yeast comes from the honey of the plant.

Once the agaves are ripe, the Jimadors use a coa (a long handled tool) to extract them from the earth. The leaves are trimmed off and the plant's heart called the piña, which looks like a pineapple, is used to make the tequila. Each piña can weigh up to 150 pounds. We perform a physical inspection of the piña to check for ripeness and disease before production.

The first step of the process is cooking or roasting in an old-fashioned clay oven called a horno for 40 hours. After the roasting, they rest for 8 hours. This is the traditional way to cook the agave, which adds more flavor.

The valves in the ovens are opened and the honeys are drained out. The first honeys produced are thrown out (too bitter). Later, the second honeys come out and they are rich in fermentable sugars and are added to the fermentation stage.

The piñas are taken to the grinding area where the honeys are separated from the fibers. The grinding process produces the agave juice known as the "most."

The formulation process is where the mosts are prepared for fermentation. (This process is part of Señor Rio's secret.) Next is fermentation, which takes 3 to 5 days. The most is stored at room temperature with no artificial heat, and it reaches full fermentation when the work of the yeast is completed.

Next is the distillation. Señor Rio is double distilled in stainless steel pot stills to keep the true essence of the agave taste. During distillation three products are obtained: heads,

which are undesirable and discarded; the heart, which comes after 2 ½ hours of distillation; and the tails which are also discarded at the end of distillation.

The first distillation of the heart is called ordinary tequila. The second distillation is called white tequila.

Ordinary tequila has an alcohol percentage of 20-28 percent, the second distillation usually has a 55-60 percent alcohol content. At this point, the tequila is diluted with demineralized water to bring it to 40 percent alcohol.

There are three basic styles known as the expressions of tequila: The Blanco, Reposado, and Añejo. Blanco can be aged up to 2 months, Reposado is aged between 2 and 12 months, and Añejo aged 1 to 3 years. The Extra Añejo can be aged for over three years.

Our Blanco is not aged; the Reposado is aged 6 months; Añejo for two years, and Extra Añejo for 5 years, all in French oak cognac barrels.

The bottling is the last stage of the process and is highly regulated by the CRT (The Tequila Reglitory Commission). Like Champagne, tequila can only be produced in these five regions: Michoacan, Nayrit, Tamaulipas, Guanajuato, and Jalisco. The state of Jalisco is where 85% of the tequilas come from. The labels must read Hecho en Mexico (Made in Mexico) unless it is a mixto tequila, which is not 100% agave and can be bottled anywhere in the world.

Señor Rio does not produce a *mixto* tequila. Señor Rio is all natural, no additives, no preservatives, gluten free, and keto friendly. *Salud!*

*To learn more, please visit:*
*www.senorrio.com*
*www.onebottleatatimebook.com*

# INDUSTRY REVIEWS

In the vast tequila landscape, we sought not only recognition through competitions but also the genuine, unfiltered opinions of industry experts and our valued customers. The reviews we garnered, like golden appraisals, became the echoes of our dedication to crafting exceptional tequila, each one a testament to the value we infused into every bottle.

*Wine Enthusiast:*
Blanco Tequila: 92 points – The striking bottle with its thick, cut glass and spicy oregano aroma set the stage. The agave sweetness, faint coconut notes, and a touch of pepper make it perfect for spicy cocktails.

Reposado Tequila: 91 points – Mild, light, and dry, with a floral flavor and smoky finish. Smooth as silk, ideal for sipping or mixing into spicy cocktails.

Añejo Tequila: 91 points – Two years of rest in cognac barrels create a mellow tequila with coconut, light smokiness, and a soft caramel flavor.

*Tequila.net:*
Blanco  89 points,
Reposado 91 points - Crafted from 100% blue Weber agaves hand harvested and roasted in traditional Stone ovens.
Añejo 93 points - Honored for its exceptional quality.

*Tequila Bob, Austin, Texas:*
Loved the clean and crisp presentation of the bottle, the agave forwardness and perfect balance of the cognac barrel won me over. The

Señor Rio Reposado is my favorite.

*Tequila Examiner:*
Blanco: Highly recommended, becoming a new favorite for margaritas.

Reposado and Añejo: Both recommended, showcasing the brand's consistent quality.

*Robert Plotkin, BarMedia:*
Each expression of Señor Rio was described as sensational, well-representing the best qualities of tequila.

*Sean Ludford, BevX.com:*
Añejo: A seriously good tequila with depth and a well-proportioned use of wood.

Reposado: A lush and silky mouthfeel focused on baked agave, herbs, and citrus.

Blanco: Crystal clear, wonderfully fruity and floral with complex flavors.

## CUSTOMER REVIEWS

"An exceptionally smooth tequila that blends flavors of citrus, vanilla, spice, and fine oak. Perfect for any occasion."

"A surprising delight with herbaceous agave aromas, a silky texture, and complex flavors finishing with a hint of Valencia orange."

"Señor Rio became a staple in the bar, appreciated for its sophisticated and smooth Blanco, making it a big hit at parties."

A discerning bartender praised the distinct taste and finishes of all three varieties, setting Señor Rio as the base for their signature margarita.

"The Añejo, described as smooth, complex, and rich, became a preferred choice over bourbon and single malt scotch."

"Tasting notes revealed fresh grass, green agave, grapefruit, white pepper, and coriander, with a sweet and spicy finish."

"The Añejo was particularly highlighted for its sense of place, capturing the earthy essence and becoming a favorite for a contemplative evening."

"The entire line of Señor Rio was celebrated for its great agave flavor, character, and smoothness, offering a dilemma between sipping or mixing in delicious cocktails."

# ACKNOWLEDGEMENTS

To my family and friends, your unwavering love, support, and belief in me have been the heartbeat of this journey.

To my daughters Crystal and Tiffany, their husbands Kevin and Paul, and my beautiful seven grandchildren, your smiles and strength inspire me every day.

To my sister, Maria, my brother-in-law, Johnny, my niece Carmella, my dear friends, and our incredible team, thank you for standing by my side through every challenge and triumph.

To my brother-in-law, Robert, and sister-in-law, Ikuko, thank you for your constant encouragement, wisdom, and guidance. Your belief in our shared vision has been a source of strength and motivation throughout the Señor Rio journey.

To my business partner, Joe Mantegna, your mentorship and support have been invaluable. Together, we have pushed boundaries and brought new energy to the brand.

And to my incredible team, none of this would be possible without your dedication, hard work, and passion. You've been the backbone of Señor Rio Tequila, and I'm grateful every day for your commitment to excellence. This journey has been extraordinary because of all of you.

Together, we've built more than just a brand; we've created a legacy rooted in family, tradition, and heart. This success is ours to celebrate.

Debbie Medina-Gach is the Co-Founder and CEO of Jalisco International Import, Inc., a minority woman-owned business that produces and owns the ultra-premium tequila brand Señor Rio Tequila. Prior to becoming a trail-blazing figure in the tequila industry, she worked for over two decades in the banking and real estate industries. During that time, Debbie developed her love of con-necting with and helping families achieve their dream of home-ownership.

Debbie, who co-founded the company with her late husband Jon-athan Gach in 2007, believes in family first and loves learning about the people who cross her path. Despite her professional success, she remains grounded in her values, shaped by a chal-lenging upbringing.

Giving back is one of the passions that lives deep in Debbie's core and, as a result, she is committed to helping others, espe-cially children, because she feels they are such a beautiful gift. Motivated by personal experiences, Debbie founded the We Care Crusade foundation to support children and families facing conditions like those of her twin granddaughters who have special needs and are her heroes. Through her work and philanthropy, she champions diversity, inclusion, and equity.

Debbie is a baby boomer, widow, and entrepreneur who believes in philanthropy, charity, and improving the lives of others. Originally from Chicago, Illinois, Debbie moved to Gilbert, Arizona, in 2000 and has two beautiful daughters. When she's not working, she loves spending time with family and friends, meeting new people, and traveling.

Her favorite quotes are:

"The best way to find yourself is to lose yourself
in the service of others."

—Gandhi

"Do unto others as you would have them do unto you."

(Matthew 7:12)

# ABOUT THE COCKTAIL CRAFTSMAN

Carlos Ruiz, a veteran of the Food and Beverage industry with over twenty-five years of hospitality experience, has made a significant impact in tequila sales and distribution across Arizona and California. His passion for spirits, especially agave, is contagious, and he consistently shares his expertise to elevate premium bar programs nationwide. Carlos excels in training bartenders, crafting cocktail menus, and hosting tastings, bringing depth and creativity to the industry.

Originally from San Diego, California, Carlos developed his foundation in classic cocktails in St. Louis before settling in Tucson, Arizona. There, he deepened his knowledge of agave spirits, blending traditional techniques with modern flair. His workshops and tequila tastings, offered in California, Arizona, Missouri, and Maine, have garnered attention from various media outlets. Carlos is proud to showcase the bold flavors and refined sophistication of blue weber agave through his educational events, leaving a lasting impact on the beverage community.

Personal Note: I wanted to contribute to this book for several meaningful reasons. It offers me the chance to be part of something we began so many years ago—those early days of sharing our passion through tequila tastings and watching our dream take root. Witnessing the growth of the brand and how Debbie has continued with hers and Jon's vision, staying true to the underdog spirit of Señor Rio tequila, fills me with pride. We've strived to create a tequila that leaves its mark on the industry, one that truly makes an impact.

For me, this is also a deeply personal way of saying goodbye to Jonathan. His legacy lives on, not only through Señor Rio, but in the hearts of everyone he touched. Jon was more than just a friend and mentor to me—he was an inspiration. His spirit will continue to resonate, as loved and cherished as ever.

## ABOUT THE PHOTOGRAPHER

A proud 5th-generation Arizonian, I'm Tara, though some know me as Nova. As the founder of Phoenix Design and Development, I've been on a creative journey since starting my digital agency at just seventeen years old. Now, at twenty-nine, my team and I have spent over a decade blending creativity and strategy to help brands thrive in the digital space. Based in Phoenix, our agency is dedicated to crafting impactful websites, innovative designs, and marketing strategies that have brought millions in revenue to clients and gained recognition across the USA.

Our work spans coast to coast, with graphic designs featured in nearly every mall in Arizona. Outside of the office, I'm fueled by adventure alongside my three loyal dogs, exploring the beauty of Arizona and beyond. Follow my journey on Instagram at @arizonataranova to see where our next adventure takes us! At Phoenix Design and Development, we're passionate about creating digital experiences that help businesses grow and supporting causes we care about.